Earl Lovelace

THE CARIBBEAN BIOGRAPHY SERIES

The Caribbean Biography Series from the University of the West Indies Press celebrates and memorializes the architects of Caribbean culture. The series aims to introduce general readers to those individuals who have made sterling contributions to the region in their chosen field – literature, the arts, politics, sports – and are the shapers and bearers of Caribbean identity.

Other Titles in This Series
Derek Walcott, by Edward Baugh
Marcus Garvey, by Rupert Lewis

EARL LOVELACE

Funso Aiyejina

The University of the West Indies Press
Jamaica • Barbados • Trinidad and Tobago

The University of the West Indies Press
7A Gibraltar Hall Road, Mona
Kingston 7, Jamaica
www.uwipress.com
© 2017, 2018 by Funso Aiyejina
All rights reserved. Published 2017

Paperback edition published 2018

A catalogue record of this book is
available from the National Library of Jamaica.
ISBN: 978-976-640-627-1 (cloth)
978-976-640-689-9 (paper)
978-976-640-628-8 (Kindle)
978-976-640-629-5 (ePub)

Cover photograph by Walt Lovelace
Cover and book design by Robert Harris
Set in Whitman 11.5/15

Printed in the United States of America

For Lynda, Abuenameh and Ararimeh: mother and sons

CONTENTS

PREFACE / ix

INTRODUCTION / 1

ONE / 7

TWO / 27

THREE / 78

NOTES / 93

BIBLIOGRAPHY / 95

ACKNOWLEDGEMENTS / 101

PREFACE

My association with Earl Lovelace dates back to my years as a doctoral student (1977–1980) at the University of the West Indies, St Augustine, Trinidad and Tobago. As a member of the University of the West Indies Players, which premiered both *Jestina's Calypso* and *The New Hardware Store* during that period, I interacted with him on the occasions when he attended our rehearsals and contributed his creator's insights to our interpretations of those plays. Kenneth Ramchand, my supervisor, would also invite me to ride along whenever he and his family and friends were going to visit Lovelace in Francis Trace, Matura. I remember the excitement of meeting Derek Walcott, Lawrence and Jenny Scott, and many other literary figures on those limes. The conversations were always charged and robust. I was new to the Caribbean and opted to embrace the wisdom of the chicken in the fiction of my people. The chicken had found itself at the gate of a strange city. It stood, pensive, on one leg, in front of the huge gate. A man chanced by and asked why it was standing on one leg. The chicken responded that it had never been to that city before and did not know the walking style in the city.

"So?"

"So, I am waiting and watching to observe the tradition of the city to know whether I should strut on both legs or hop on one."

I was a chicken on one foot, standing. Listening. Observing. Cautious. Not even in the cricket by the beach that they played often did I fully participate. Cricket is an elitist sport in Nigeria. I did not go to a prestige school. I do not play cricket.

Two things stand out for me from those years. The first is the legendary electricity-powered refrigerator in the Lovelaces' home. There was, as yet, no electricity in that part of Matura. In the absence of electricity, Lovelace pressed the refrigerator into higher intellectual service. He stored his books and manuscripts in it. I never did get the story about why he bought an electric fridge when there was no electricity to run it. Maybe it was an expression of faith – faith that, one day, one day, the government was bound to extend the service to Francis Trace. The kind of prediction you can bank, once it does not come with an expiry date. The other thing I remember from those days is Jean Lovelace's legendary home-made wine – cashew wine, grapefruit wine, pommecythere wine, pommerac wine, rice wine, sorrel wine. . . . The list was endless.

I returned to Nigeria at the end of 1980 to continue my university teaching career at my alma mater, Obafemi Awolowo University, Ile-Ife, and took over the teaching of

West Indian literature. As an undergraduate at Ile-Ife, I had studied West Indian literature as a component of Commonwealth literature, and the offering had been limited to V.S. Naipaul, George Lamming and Kamau Brathwaite. I now had the opportunity to teach a whole course on West Indian literature. The first book I added to the list was Lovelace's *The Dragon Can't Dance*. As I suspected, because of its engagement with the manifestation of Africa in the New World, the book was hugely popular with students. They reacted to it with the same zeal that my generation of undergraduates had reacted to Kamau Brathwaite's *Masks*.

One of the first hurdles I faced when I set about to read, study and, later, teach Lovelace was the unavailability of his views outside of his fictive constructs. In an attempt to understand the man and his work, I started from early o'clock to collect his non-fiction writings. I visited Trinidad and Tobago about once every two years between 1981 and my final relocation there in 1989; and every time I visited, I collected any materials about him and by him that I could find. Then, in 1994, I approached him with a proposal to edit a selection of his essays for publication in order to obviate the difficulty faced by students and scholars in locating them. He was receptive to the suggestion. Soon after, I took possession of a boxful of some of his papers. This box contained manuscripts of some of the columns he had written for the *Trinidad Express* between 1967 and 1969, reviews, speeches, and versions of partially written pieces on a range of issues. Many of them contained copious handwritten marginalia waiting to be integrated or rejected.

PREFACE

Between 1996 and 2001, when I was the assistant editor of the *Trinidad and Tobago Review*, I initiated a system by which I secured copies of Lovelace's speeches, as soon after their delivery as possible, for publication in that journal. With the active collaboration of his children, I kept track of his speaking engagements and would be literally waiting in the wings to collect copies of his speeches from him as soon as he was finished. When they were foreign engagements, I made sure I found myself at his home as soon as he returned so that I could secure copies. Even when he insisted that the talks were incomplete, I would insist on the incomplete versions. By then, on the basis of the number of incomplete pieces in that boxful of papers I had collected from him, I had come to realize that once he had delivered a speech, often partly written and partly improvised, he hardly ever returned to it. He would rather return his attention to a novel-in-progress than to the task of refining a talk that he had already delivered. However, once I had a version of a speech, it was always much easier to get him to talk through the blanks, to refine, clarify, expand or modify, over a drink of cocoa, sweetened with condensed milk and spiked with grated nutmeg – a Lovelace special.

The process was slow because I had to work to suit his schedule, in addition to having to navigate his not-so-legible handwriting. Finally, in 2003, *Growing in the Dark* was published. This selection of his essays, speeches and notes towards his autobiography spans from 1967 to 2000, and confirms Lovelace as one of the most consistent and perceptive organic and original thinkers, writers and cultural workers from the Caribbean. This biography would not have been possible, at least not in this form, had *Growing in the Dark* not happened.

Long before the conception of the Caribbean Biography Series and the selection of Lovelace as one of its subjects, I had started a series of formal and informal interviews with him with a view to creating a body of secondary materials for teaching his books to my students, especially students in the Advanced Seminar on West Indian Literature (Earl Lovelace).

A lot of the personal details of his life in this book come from a number of sources: (1) from the many hours of my recorded interviews with him; (2) from years of informal chats with him; with Jean, his wife; with Lyris, his sister; and with Jim Armstrong and Eddie Hernandez, his friends; (3) from the autobiographical references in his essays, especially "Working Obeah", in *Growing in the Dark*; (4) from the manuscript of his autobiography-in-progress; and (5) from the Earl Lovelace Manuscripts housed at the Alma Jordan Library, the University of the West Indies, St Augustine, Trinidad and Tobago.

Funso Aiyejina
Five Rivers, Arouca/Asetu Forest Sanctuary, Narangho, Cumana, Toco
Trinidad and Tobago
September 2016

INTRODUCTION

Earl Wilbert Lovelace has the distinction of being one of the few West Indian writers of his generation to have lived in, and written from, the region at a time when metropolitan exile was the more attractive and lucrative option. In his journey from being a new writer in 1964 to becoming a nationally and internationally celebrated writer today, Lovelace has worked as forest ranger, agricultural assistant, proofreader, journalist, resident playwright and director of grassroots theatre groups, and university lecturer. No matter what he did, he remained an avid reader of books and an astute student of people, in preparation for, or in continuation of, his commitment to the writing of Trinidad and Tobago and the Caribbean; primarily, but not exclusively, for the benefit of the region. His focus has been a desire to make people appreciate the meaning of their humanity. Hence, he has consistently addressed the issues of the multiple identities (sometimes antagonistic, other times complementary) that drive multicultural societies like the Caribbean; the responsibility of the self to the community; and the obligations of the community to its constituents, especially those who have been disadvantaged by the realities of enslavement, indentureship, colonialism and the failures of their postcolonial leaders.

Lovelace articulates people's desire to belong, their need to claim and understand their landscapes and the intricacies of their histories, and the impulse to recognize the human dignity inherent in their unique contexts, complete with their beauty and their follies. He champions the culture and language of the folk (the ordinary people, as he calls them), whom he envisions as the most instinctive and versatile bearers and creators of culture in the Caribbean; and he is as persistent in his commitment to craft as he is compassionate in his presentation of his characters and the landscapes of their struggles for self-apprehension and self-realization. This compassion is born out of his self-identification with the rural dwellers among whom he lived and worked – men and women who demonstrated their love of life and their awareness that individuals must be responsible for the world they inhabit. It is this philosophical conditioning that directs Lovelace's abiding passion for creating fictions in which the multiplicity of voices and perspectives within his multicultural being and enabling communities are democratically ventilated.

Lovelace has emerged as one of the leading writers from the Caribbean, both from the point of view of thematic relevance as well as the novelty of his style. He has garnered national and international prizes, including the BP Independence Literary Prize (1964) for the manuscript of his first novel, *While Gods Are Falling*; the Commonwealth Writers' Prize (1997) and a shortlisting for the International IMPAC Dublin Literary Prize (1998) for *Salt*; and the Grand Prize for Caribbean Literature (from the Regional Council of Guadeloupe) and the OCM Bocas Prize for Caribbean Literature for *Is Just a Movie* (2011, 2012 respectively). His other publications include *The Schoolmaster* (1968), *The Dragon Can't Dance* (1979), *The Wine of Astonishment* (1982), *Jestina's Calypso and Other Plays* (1984), *A Brief Conversion and Other Stories* (1988), and *Crawfie the Crapaud* (a children's story, 1997). He has adapted *The Wine of Astonishment* and *The Dragon Can't Dance* for the stage. His original plays and the adapted ones have been performed in the Caribbean, the United Kingdom and the United States. He has also adapted his short story "Joebell and America" for the screen. His works have been translated into several languages including German, French, Dutch, Hungarian and Japanese.

In 1982, *The Wine of Astonishment* caused a minor protocol crisis for the Trinidad and Tobago high commissioner to the United Kingdom. On 20 April, Lovelace was in London to launch *The Wine of Astonishment* at the First International Black Radical Book Fair. The legendary radical thinker C.L.R. James, who had been very supportive of his literary career, was in London specifically for the launch of the book. The launch was followed by a reception at the official residence of the Trinidad and Tobago high commissioner on 27 April. Many wondered whether the exiled C.L.R. James would be allowed into the residence of the high commissioner. To the delight of many, the "Trinidad and Tobago High

Commissioner, Mr. Eustace Seignoret, opened the doors of his 'auspicious offices' and allowed the exiled veteran politician C.L.R. James, a grand entrance". The *Trinidad Guardian* of 9 May 1982 did not miss the significance of the occasion: "It was an emotional evening for the frail and past 80 C.L.R. who thanked the High Commissioner for his gesture and was obviously enthralled with the opportunity to meet and talk with friends. . . . He told the gathering that Lovelace is one of the foremost writers in the Caribbean today, on the path of national consciousness, telling the world who we are and taking our rightful place in society."

In recognition of Lovelace's contribution to literature and culture, he has been conferred with several national and international awards over the years. He got the Pegasus Literary Award for his outstanding contribution to the arts in Trinidad and Tobago (November 1965); a Guggenheim Fellowship (1980, which facilitated his visit to the International Writing Program at the University of Iowa, United States); Trinidad and Tobago's Chaconia Medal (Gold, 1988); honorary doctor of letters from the University of the West Indies, St Augustine (2002); and the President's Medal from the Pacific Lutheran University, Tacoma, United States (2014). In August 1995, when he was honoured at CARIFESTA VI, alongside Ernest Moutoussamy, Rex Nettleford, V.S. Naipaul, Derek Walcott, Kamau Brathwaite, Martin Carter, George Lamming and Sylvia Wynter, he was toasted by Gordon Rohlehr, in his citation, as "a tireless worker and an inspiring energy [who] has retained and transmitted in lyrical moving prose his intimate feeling for the common rural folk and their bewildered descendants who have tried to reconstruct a kind of life in the yards and dusty ghettoes of our cities". In 1997, on the heels of winning the Commonwealth Writers' Prize for *Salt*, he was awarded the "*Express* Individual of the Year". In 2005, he was appointed to the Board of Governors of the University of Trinidad and Tobago; and in 2006, when Trinidad and Tobago hosted CARIFESTA IX, he was appointed its artistic director. In 2011, he was inducted into the Tobago Literary Hall of Fame. To mark the fiftieth anniversary of the independence of Trinidad and Tobago in 2012, Lovelace was bestowed with a Lifetime Literary Award by the National Library and Information System Authority of Trinidad and Tobago.

When Lovelace turned seventy in July 2005, the University of the West Indies at St Augustine acknowledged and celebrated him as a sensitive narrator of the nation and its people. Recognizing that the celebration of a man of the people like Lovelace could not and should not be restricted to the ivory tower, "Lovelace@70" was conceptualized and executed as a series of community-based, stakeholder-driven events. Hence, although the initiative for the conference and celebrations originated from the St Augustine campus, Lovelace scholars from the Cave Hill and Mona campuses as well as from the University of Miami and Pacific Lutheran University (Tacoma, Washington) – two of the American universities with which he had had significant intellectual relationships – were specially invited to participate. Also, as a result of the decision not to limit the celebrations to the academy, the various local communities in which Lovelace had worked and about which he had written were invited to take charge of specific aspects of the celebrations, with the university retaining only a coordinating role in those activities that were not under its direct remit.[1]

ONE

Earl Lovelace was born on 13 July 1935 in Toco, Trinidad, to Jane Wattley and Simon Lovelace. He remembers his mother as an individual imbued with a sense of adventure and a rebellious spirit. By the time she left Tobago on a schooner for Toco in Trinidad, the young and unmarried Jane had already had one daughter (Lillian) and two sons (John and Talbot). Her departure from Tobago, with John, her older son, in tow, was precipitated by, in addition to her desire to escape the fundamentalist strictures of her Methodist father, the sudden death of the father of John and Talbot, an estate overseer from St Kitts.

On her arrival in Toco, Jane took a job at Patience Estate as a cook. She subsequently met and fell in love with Simon Lovelace, the son of landowning Cecilia Moniquette and John Lovelace. Jane and Simon lived together and had two children, a girl (Lyris) and Earl, before their separation and her move from Toco to Rio Claro.

In addition to her sense of adventure, Lovelace remembers his mother, although he did not grow up with her, as "a very tender special person" whose "principal gift was love" (personal interview, 2005). At age three, his mother took him to Tobago and placed him, like his cousins, under the care of his maternal grandparents (Eva Wattley, a Black Carib from Chateaubelair in St Vincent, and Moses Wattley, a Tobagonian) in Calder Hall, Scarborough. He lived in Tobago until age eleven when he returned, ostensibly, to his mother in Trinidad but would, on his mother's request, live with his grandmother and later with his aunt Lorna before moving to live with his mother.

His maternal grandparents were active members of the Methodist Church, and the young Lovelace and his cousins were required to attend with them. His grandfather was a dominant presence and force, a man with a sense of self and a belief in the rightness of his own ways. In his house,

> there were two activities, at least for adults: Work and Church. My grandfather collected the collection in the Scarborough Methodist Church and we went with him every Sunday. In the week, he worked in his garden on land he had at Old Fort, planting plantains, cassava, cocoa, and avocadoes. On Saturdays I went with my grandmother to the market where she sold sweetbread and tarts. She made jams, etc. We had chickens and goats and a cow. Now and again my grandfather would go to the races in Trinidad. But in the house we couldn't sing calypso, nobody played mas, Carnival; these were activities of the Devil.[2]

Lovelace would later immortalize his grandfather in the figure of the grandfather in *The Dragon Can't Dance*, where he is fictionalized as stern and stiff and unbending, the pillar of a falling building, whose slightest shift would collapse the entire structure . . . this man, his mother's father, . . . still holding on then to five acres of mountain and stone that had exhausted its substance, if it ever had any, years before he bought it, holding on with a passion so fierce that it blinded him to the dwindling size of the fruit the tired brown tree tugged out of the earth, as if the land, the mountain and the stone land, held some promise that he alone knew of, that was never revealed to his wife or to his children, and that would be already lost to Aldrick by the time he was old enough to understand. (36–37)

Lovelace remembers Calder Hall as the nursery for his grandparents' grandchildren. When he got to Tobago, he joined his eldest sister and the brother before him as well as his two cousins who were the same age as him. He bonded with the first family and relatives with whom he would have "a closeness that nothing could displace and even though now I do not see them as often as I believe I should, there is that something that roots me, roots us" (Lovelace, autobiography-in-progress, hereafter cited in text as AIP).

In addition to his grandparents, sister, brother and cousins in that immediate family circle, he recalls, very fondly, Aunt Lorna, who worked as a clerk at Miller Store; Aunt Elaine, who was a nurse at the Scarborough Hospital; Aunt Ina; and Uncle Cecil – his mother's brother (the father of his two cousins, Wilbert and Alford), who was a stevedore on the Port of Spain wharf and used to religiously send boxes of foodstuff to them by the boat from Trinidad every week.

The Tobago experience provided Lovelace with "a balance

sheet of benefits as a nursery of love and an anchor of generosity and caring" that prepared him "to engage the world". At about five or six, he contracted typhoid fever. While at the Scarborough Hospital, convinced that he was going to die, he started to recite the names of his relatives. He wanted to remember them before he died. That desire to remember would become a central pillar in his performance as a writer, committed to the process of re-memorizing the past into a talisman for confronting the present. He recovered from the typhoid and had to learn to walk all over again. As a result of his susceptibility to illness, his grandparents rarely called on him to perform manual tasks. Unlike his cousins, he had "a passport to a life of ease" which "left him free to read" (Lovelace, AIP).

In his grandparents' house, there was a range of books, especially English literature and books on African Americans, which fascinated him and set him on the path of becoming an avid reader. After exhausting the books at home, he turned to the Scarborough Public Library.

Lovelace began formal schooling at the Scarborough Methodist Primary School in Tobago (1940–1947). But before going to primary school, he attended a nursery school a few yards from his grandparents' home in Calder Hall. He remembers reading a Mother Goose book about a "duck leading its ducklings to a pond, [a] hen gathering its fluffy chickens under its wings [and] the cock, with its red crown and splendid tail feathers, parading somewhere at the margin of the page" (Lovelace, AIP) at this school. But, more important, for the adult that Lovelace would become, he remembers taking part in a game of the Farmer in the Dell which left such an indelible mark on his personality that he regularly references it as an adult.

Lovelace watched anxiously as the child who had appropriated the role of the Farmer picked a wife from among the other children. The Wife picked their Child. Their Child picked the Dog. The Dog picked the Cat and the Cat picked the Rat. With only one role left, the young Lovelace watched anxiously, afraid he would not get a role in the play. Mercifully, the Rat picked him for the role of the Cheese. He was the Cheese who would not get to choose anyone and who would stand alone and be the first victim in the game – the one to be eaten by the Rat before the Rat is eaten by the Cat. That experience would manifest in the adult Lovelace a capacity to identify with the marginalized, the underprivileged – the victimized and ill-used, the overlooked, the underdogs, the cheeses of this world. If most of his fictional protagonists tend to be from the lower stratum of society, it is precisely because of that early childhood exposure to being given the least important role – a role with neither power nor responsibility. There is a sense in which the creative and critical vision that Lovelace went on to develop and articulate was inspired in part by the plight of the cheese in that schoolyard play. The castaway, the alienated, the rebel and the underprivileged would become central to his fictive constructs – the rebellious Walter Castle in *While Gods Are Falling*, the exploited villagers in *The Schoolmaster*, the oppressed Spiritual Baptist community in *The Wine of Astonishment*, the Gang of Nine in *The Dragon Can't Dance*,

Bango in *Salt*, and Sonnyboy in *Is Just a Movie*, to name the major ones.

By age ten, he had read all the books available in the house and was well "on his way to a pleasant middleclass existence which I was going to achieve by becoming a doctor (every child was going to become a doctor) and this I would embark upon when I passed the college exhibition examination which I would sit at age eleven".³

In the process of his reading, the young Lovelace started to notice the details of history that never formed part of the conversations the adults engaged in at home (his grandfather was more disposed to talking about his disputations with Reverend Harrison, the white priest in charge of the Methodist Church, than talking about politics or history of Tobago, all the more to underscore his intellectual parity with the reverend). Lovelace's reading exposed him to the struggles of African Americans, through whom he began to see a counter to the Spanish heritage that he had been told was his inheritance from his paternal line. At this point, too, he started to question the absence of images of himself in the books he read. He was confused: "I was looking to the Black side and that made the idea of belonging to slaves problematic. But having chosen to identify with this side of my ancestry, I had to accept that I belonged to those people called slaves. So there I was, on the one hand 'Spanish' that had abandoned me and on the other, Negro – these people who I was introduced to as slaves" (Lovelace, AIP).

This was the beginning of his political consciousness, even though it was happening in an unstructured manner:

CHAPTER ONE

> I was eleven in 1946, the year of Adult Franchise. The day after the elections, I sat down at the table on which my grandmother ironed clothes and underlined on the newspaper all the black people that had won seats in the elections. In Tobago, APT James beat Captain Harrower, an Englishman; I looked at Butler, Pope McLean, Victor Bryan won in Eastern counties. . . . I supported Butler and hoped that he would win the elections. That must have been the beginning of my interest in politics. I never quite worked out where that interest came from. My reading? My grandfather? The newspapers? And what made me a supporter of Butler? My grandmother's discussion of the novels she read? (Lovelace, AIP)

Lovelace was considered an academically bright child, seen by many as the one marked out for escape from the ordinariness of their life into an alternative and better world of the educated elites. Throughout the course of his primary school in Tobago, he consistently placed first or second in tests. Everyone expected him to pass the college exhibition examination with flying colours and be on his way to a middle-class existence as a doctor. In 1947, at age eleven, he sat the examination and, to his and others' horror, he failed. He was devastated. But, luckily, he still had another chance at the examination to redeem himself.

In 1948, Lovelace left Tobago to return to Trinidad with his grandmother, Aunt Lorna and his cousins. His grandmother's marriage had collapsed at this point. In Trinidad, his cousins went to live with their father. But Lovelace continued to live with his grandmother and, later, with Aunt Lorna in Belmont. To make sure of his success in the college exhibition examination in his second and final attempt, Lovelace, who was brought up as a Methodist in Tobago, was enrolled at the Nelson Street Boys' School, a Catholic school that was famous for producing successful scholarship winners.

But before this all-important examination, there was the matter of settling into Trinidad. He had been excited about the prospect of returning home. In Tobago, he saw himself as a Trinidadian; he romanticized Trinidad as his birthplace, his paternal island. But he would learn on his return to Trinidad that there was more to belonging than blood ties:

> As a child, I did not feel Tobagonian. I was something of an outsider there. Trinidad was bigger, grander: I claimed my Trinidadian paternity. When years later I returned to Trinidad, talking with the accent of a Tobagonian, the first thing an arrogant little Trinidadian boy said to me was, "Hey, Baje," calling me a Barbadian. I realise that if I was a stranger in Tobago, this place, Trinidad, was not as fully mine as I had thought; I was a stranger here too.[4]

Lovelace saw this experience as another confirmation of his Otherness, an echo of the cheese-that-stood-alone episode from his nursery school year. Rather than correct the boy who had called him a Barbadian, Lovelace stepped back, mentally, and started to re-examine his notion of Trinidad as home. He came to a realization that he could claim neither Tobago nor Trinidad as home. The processes and rituals of belonging would become major motifs in both his life and his writing. This experience would inspire in him an

CHAPTER ONE

insider/outsider complex, a quality of character that makes it possible for him to simultaneously examine contexts in which he is deeply invested with the dispassionate gaze of an impartial outsider and to interrogate situations that are foreign to him with the compassion of a committed native. He would later deploy this understanding of the creative ambiguity/complexity inherent in Otherness to construct multi-visioned and multi-versioned approaches to life, and to simultaneously delineate characters and themes that are realized through a complex interplay of both the perspectives of the Insider and those of the Outsider. Nowhere is this possibility more evident than in *Salt*, where Lovelace succeeds in entering sympathetically and critically into the minds of enslavers and the enslaved, and in *The Dragon Can't Dance*, where his African characters are as complex and conflicted as his Indian characters. He articulates the view that people are not simply victims or victors, guilty or guiltless, exploiters or exploited. They are, first and foremost, people.

The episode of his misclassification as a foreigner in Trinidad on his return from Tobago had another significant impact on Lovelace. It would become his metaphor for the need to understand that, over and beyond biological rights, every individual must earn the right to belong to a community, and that you need to take time to know people before you can say that you know them. This would have fuelled his enthusiastic and wholehearted immersion in the life of the various communities in which he has settled, especially Valencia, Rio Claro, Tobago and Matura.

Another early lesson for Lovelace on his arrival in Trinidad from Tobago was his discovery that, just as it was the case in Tobago, there was no one with whom he could share his love of books and his emerging radical consciousness of history and politics. He had hoped that Trinidad, being the bigger place, would have had people who were raising the same questions he had been raising with himself about history and politics. But that was not to be. So, the young Lovelace was left with no option but to keep his storehouse of knowledge and consciousness to himself, a hidden treasure:

> If I was set apart from my fellows, it was because of this secret place, this place where I was accumulating this history, gathering up ideas of who we were, of who I was, of where we had come from. And while it was important to me, it was not as urgent as it might have been because no one around me seemed to be quite as interested. Not that they did not want this knowledge but because they did not know what they would do with it, and without this communal acknowledgement of its value, this accumulating of details of a history and a perspective on it became a private enterprise to me, something in its own compartment. (Lovelace, AIP)

In the first test he sat at Nelson Street Boys' School, he placed in a shocking ninth position. This was a far cry from the first or, at worse, second place position to which he was accustomed at the Scarborough Methodist School in Tobago. After that test, his performance got progressively worse, until he would have been ecstatic to regain that shocking ninth position.

There were mitigating factors for his low performance in

school. He had left the solidity of family in Tobago for a less stable existence in Trinidad. His mother, who had separated from his father when he was about six years old, had moved from Toco to St James via Rio Claro and was financially challenged. Because of the "difficult circumstances in which she lived with four children, the one after me, a girl, afflicted with polio" (Lovelace, AIP), his mother had asked her sister to "take" Earl when he returned to Trinidad from Tobago. But no sooner had he settled to a rhythm at the home of Aunt Lorna and begun to plot a path to improving his academic standing in his new school than his mother asked him to choose between living with her and living with his aunt. He was called upon to choose between a loving aunt who had no children of her own and who had lovingly treated her sister's children as hers, and a mother for whom he felt love but with whom he had not lived since he was three. He chose his mother. The adult Lovelace reflects:

> Now as I think of it, I see how devastating it must have been for Aunt Lorna. How much of a traitor I must have seemed. I loved Aunt Lorna dearly and I loved my mother. I chose to go to live with my mother. It hurt Lorna. . . . She didn't even talk about it. Let me choose. You want to go by your mother? How it must have hurt her. Go. But what was I choosing between? Now it seems clear to me. I had been "given" to Lorna. I had left the poor woman and had been given to a better-off relative, given love, school, everything that they could afford. I would have been the son she never had but the one she made of me. She must have been sure of my love. . . . Somewhere in the middle of this preparation for the exhibition examination, I

> left Lorna and went to live with my mother and the rest of the family in Morvant. I had been required to choose in a situation in which any choice was the wrong choice. (Lovelace, AIP)

Lovelace would affirm the depth of his love for Aunt Lorna in 1964 when he dedicated *While Gods Are Falling* to "my wife Jean and my aunt Lorna".

If the move to live with his mother achieved nothing else, it achieved the very fundamental introduction of Lovelace to an essential node of cultural growth that had hitherto been outside of his orbit. His mother, demonstrating the same rebellious spirit that had propelled her to leave Tobago, took the young Lovelace to a Spiritual Baptist ceremony, and it was there that he would catch a glimpse of the spirit of Africa from which his Methodist upbringing in Tobago had cut him off:

> One night my mother took me with her to a service in the Spiritual Baptist church. My mother was something of a renegade – perhaps being in Trinidad made her one; maybe she needed deeper spiritual guidance than was afforded her in the other religions. She quietly wanted to be a Spiritual Baptist. . . .
>
> The church that the coloniser had done so much to discourage was alive. The darkness had not gone away. It had been officially banned, but people had kept it on as they had kept on stickfighting in the countryside, dancing at wakes, singing at wakes. As I was to discover when I went to the countryside to live and work, they had kept up the drum, changing it first to tamboo bamboo and later to the steel drum against which there was also great resistance.[5]

But this story is getting ahead of itself.

CHAPTER ONE

Before the visit to the Spiritual Baptist church and its consequences, Lovelace had the college exhibition examination to conquer. When he finally sat the examination for the second and last time, he failed.

Strange as it may sound, Lovelace has expressed a sense of gratitude at this second failure. His gratitude derived from his realization that his first failure had nothing to do with his location in the so-called backwoods of Tobago during his first attempt at the examination. The second failure also equalized the two islands in his psyche. He failed in Tobago and failed in Trinidad. He was a stranger in Tobago and a stranger in Trinidad. This second failure put paid to his chance of going to a prestige school and the possibility of becoming a doctor. This failure would also become the first in a series of events that would conspire to keep him grounded, or trapped, in Trinidad and Tobago and with the ordinary people, thereby forcing him to grow to become one of the best students and narrators of the Caribbean from the standpoint of the not-so-privileged.

After that second failure at the college exhibition examination, Lovelace was faced with the dilemma of what to do. His mother was ailing and his father, who had left the family land in Toco to work as the caretaker of the health office in Morvant, could not afford the money for his private secondary school education. In light of the financial situation, Lovelace's mother suggested he "go and learn a trade". He "felt as if someone had punched me in the stomach. I understood the situation, but I felt as if my life had come to an end" (Lovelace,

AIP). His response demonstrates how much he had become a victim of an education system that conditioned its products to be disdainful of the working class. This also confirms that his happiness at his failures came much later in life, with the benefit of hindsight. It was only later in life, as he lived and worked among villagers and gained a better understanding of their culture and work ethos, that he would begin to appreciate and to celebrate them as the salt of the earth. Lovelace was saved from the "humiliation" of going to learn a trade, as his mother had suggested, because, once more, his maternal family came to his rescue. They found a way to pay for him to go to a private secondary school.

He was initially enrolled at a private secondary school in Morvant run by one Mr Nelson, who taught all the subjects offered in the school. What Lovelace remembers about that school (his stay there was very brief) is not what he learned or did not learn but the prediction that Mr Nelson made about his lifespan. Mr Nelson predicted that Lovelace would die at thirty! Lovelace was so shocked and worried about the prediction that, although he was not sure that he had heard correctly, he did not dare to ask and have it repeated and confirmed. He consoled himself with the thought that Mr Nelson was not a "real seer-man" and that "it was a kind of joke. That was his prediction. It was not a great number; still, it was far away from 13. As I grew closer to thirty, I would begin to remember his prediction. And I began to contemplate death. Consoling myself with the idea that we do not know when we die. Death is for others, not for the dead" (Lovelace, AIP).

CHAPTER ONE

Years later, long after he had lived past thirty and had established himself as a writer, his older brother, John, would recall another prediction, this time by a sadhu, a Hindu holy man. One blistering afternoon in Earl's infancy, a wandering sadhu had stopped by their house in Toco for a drink of water. On seeing their mother with baby Earl, the sadhu had asked to hold him. She handed the child to the sadhu and he looked into the child's eyes and read the future they reflected. "Take care of this child," he announced. "Take care of this child. This child will make you proud. He will be a good man for the world" (Lovelace, AIP). Lovelace's journey to the fulfilment of this first prophecy, and not the one by Mr Nelson, is the subject of this story.

Lovelace left Mr Nelson's "one-teacher, no-real-seer-man" school for Ideal High School on Oxford Street in Port of Spain where Mr E.L. Ellis, BA London, held sway as the principal. No science subjects were taught at Ideal High School; so, if you wanted to be a doctor, this was not your ideal school. In addition to the built-in career restrictions, the social structures in effect in the country did not facilitate social or academic interactions between students of third-tier schools like Ideal High School and successful college exhibition students (the ones "on exhibition") who went to prestige schools. They would, therefore, grow up seeing themselves and their society through different prisms, with the students of the third-tier schools feeling marginalized and more prone to embrace rebellion. Many of them would end up applying to join the police force or the regiment or excelling in sports.

This was also the period of his mother's illness and that fateful trip to the Spiritual Baptist church. In another more detailed recollection of that eye-opening trip, Lovelace reveals:

> My mother wanted to be a Shouter. Something in it called out to her. Maybe it was her illness. I was 14. It was the year before she would die. . . . It was as if as she approached what would eventually become her death, she knew and understood the value of this thing that she had been turned against all her life. She turned now and started to look to the church. But I think it was to something bigger, to some centre for herself, the spiritual centre that she had not found elsewhere. She had held out, had postponed her entry as long as she could. But now she was going. And she took me with her so that I should be a witness to her good intentions, which at some future date she would pursue.[6]

But Lovelace would become a witness to much more than his mother's good intentions. He would witness the light inside the African darkness. He would witness the invisible and unnamed spirit of Africa come alive inside that simple place of worship:

> That night a girl from the neighbourhood appeared in the church. She had been recently baptised and was now coming off the moaning/mourning ground. She must have been about 15. And she was brought in with a band over her eyes to tell the church of her travels, of her journey in the spirit. She was in white. Even now I experience again that night and the thick energy exuded by that girl as she cried and laughed and danced and screamed as she relived her journey into the regions of the dream/spirit world, telling where she had been, the rivers she had crossed, the people she had met, speaking in tongues, in

> languages, that night, flooding the church with the electricity of a transfiguring power that drew other devotees in, moving them to their own dancing and screams and their own languages, making me feel that more of a stranger, that more distant, remote from what I had no fear of. I was not afraid. It was something I had no way to embrace as much as I wanted to. I did not know it then, but I had visited the darkness that the light had kept from me.[7]

Although this was a transformative experience, Lovelace could not fully inhabit it. The girl might have switched on a light but Lovelace had not opened his eyes. It was not that he was afraid of the experience (he was there with his mother, after all), but that he felt like a stranger. His education had taught him to regard this light as darkness. It had alienated him from this reality that his mother had finally arrived at as the likely place of her salvation – spiritual salvation. He was ambivalent about belonging to the space. He had an elsewhere to aspire to, since, in spite of his failure in the college exhibition examination, he was now in high school and, unlike the girl returning from her spiritual journey or his mother seeking a spiritual home, he was still eligible for some degree of escape through his now-in-progress third-tier education. It would take two more future failures (the failure of his sister, who subsequently left for London, to send for him in 1954 as she had promised and his unsatisfactory performance in one of the subjects for his diploma in forestry in 1962, which scuttled his second attempt to go away to study) to make Lovelace begin to seriously embrace the light in that darkness and to draw on its resources to grow.

Coupled with the feeling of being a stranger in the African space in the new world to which his mother had taken him, Lovelace did not have the language to describe the experience, both then and years later:

> I recall this inadequately, I feel, because I do not have the words to describe the ceremony, its truth. This inadequacy tells of the difficulty of describing that darkness. If there are no words, then it doesn't exist, which ought to bring us to the idea that language is not a faculty by which we describe what we identify, but also one which describes what we already know, what the language already knows; which brings us to the problem that we have adopted a language which does not embrace our experiences and which cannot describe it and which we still must use to reclaim things that it knows nothing about.[8]

Lovelace has spent his writing career refining language into a medium that is capable of expressing such submerged essences in the New World, a language capable of naming the unnamed and unnameable. Reflecting on the relationship between Africans and West Indians and the English language, he asserts that "in the Caribbean, we have the need to make English our own, to make it speak for us; because it is the only language we have. Our craft involves wrestling it into shape so that it can express our distinct sensibility, a sensibility that owes something to Africa as well as our engagement with our Caribbean reality."[9] This understanding of the ideological function of language explains why he would alight on the bacchanal tradition of Trinidad and Tobago as the source inspiration for the language of narration and the language of interactions in his novels and the overall framing of his aesthetics, so much so that his novels have been dubbed "singing novels" or "novelypsoes".[10]

In 1951, Lovelace's mother died. Two years later, his father died. With the death of Jane, the younger of her children split up to live with Lillian, the eldest, and John, her second child, both of whom were now employed. Earl shuttled between John and Lillian.

Lovelace sat the Senior Cambridge Examination in 1953 and passed with a Grade 3. But much more than the certificate, it was his out-of-class experiences while attending Ideal High School that would significantly influence his growth into an adult with an understanding of the psychology of the society. During those years, he developed an interest in fetes (sometimes, joining his schoolmates to gate-crash); in pan (watching from a distance, afraid of the violence that, to a large extent, defined the pan fraternity); and in sports, especially football and cricket, both as a player and as a spectator. Lovelace was making his way

> among friends, fellows who aspired to better their positions and to have a good time. We had our limes, sitting sometimes for hours in front the shop on Duke Street, we heard about steelband riots, about gang warfare, but we were out of it. We watched the police pass in the Black Maria, the business of cleaning up gangs, all this we took to be legitimate activities since we too lived in fear of them, but we could not help but see how the innocent were being harassed, how on the streets which we felt we had a right to, we could be harassed by the police. Did we make any connection between the poverty and

neglect of these areas with the gang violence? I am not sure we did. We were busy depending on our luck and education, on our will to succeed. We were concerned with our own individual efforts to transcend our surroundings. (Lovelace, AIP)

TWO

The arrival of Eric Williams on the political scene in 1956 marked, for Lovelace, the beginning of serious and comprehensive public-level discussions of the issues around history, culture, identity, and Caribbean civilization on the whole that he had been having with himself, in the privacy of his mind, since his childhood days in Tobago. He joined many young people to welcome and participate in the public education that was at the core of Eric Williams's political ascendancy. Although enthusiastic about the vision of Eric Williams and his People's National Movement, Lovelace would grow critical of the policies and praxes of Eric Williams and the party, as evidenced in his portrayal of both in his creative works. The first concrete affirmation of his subsequent disenchantment with Eric Williams and the People's National Movement would be his association with the opposition Liberal Party led by Peter Farquhar in Tobago. In 1966, just before he left Tobago for the United States to attend Howard University, he had a fleeting association with the Liberal Party, which had considered fielding him on its slate of candidates. However, with his departure for the United States, the party fielded his friend, Eddie Hernandez, instead, against A.N.R. Robinson in Tobago East. Hernandez lost to Robinson but took pride in not losing his deposit (Jim Armstrong, e-mail, 2 September 2016).

The nature of Lovelace's relationship with Eric Williams and the People's National Movement after the initial euphoria is also evident in his subsequent participation in the 1970 Black Power movement. But, again, this story is getting too far ahead of itself.

So, back to 1953.

After passing the Senior Cambridge Examination, he needed a job. His brother, John, now a policeman, spoke to somebody at the *Guardian* and he was given a job in the proofreading department as a copy boy. For one who had developed a special affinity for words and language through his voracious appetite for reading, this was an ideal job, once he got past the overpowering smell of printing ink. But he did not last long in the job. He fell out with his supervisor, on the grounds that the supervisor spoke to him in a disrespectful tone: "We fell out once when he asked me to hand him a copy. I didn't like how he spoke to me. I thought it was disrespectful and I refused to hand him the copy. He said, 'If you do not, you will be fired.' I refused. So I was fired" (Lovelace, AIP).

This episode marked another defining moment in Lovelace's life. His behaviour would be considered impulsive and wrongheaded by many, especially since he had no guarantee of another job. Lovelace, however, saw that moment as representing "what I stood for, of who I thought I was and

CHAPTER TWO

the upholding of my own sense of my dignity. I had nothing. I had no other means and I said, 'No.' And I was rewarded by being forced to look for another job" (Lovelace, AIP).

Soon after his dismissal from the *Guardian*, he responded to an advertisement for forest rangers/forest guards and, to his surprise and relief, he was selected. This career change was the beginning of a tectonic shift in Lovelace's view of the world, a change that would not have been possible had he stayed on at the *Guardian*. Working out of Port of Spain, he would have likely been socialized into middle-class behaviours and sensibilities at the beginning of his adult life. The new job took him "away from Port of Spain and put me in the place that I would begin to be free" (Lovelace, AIP). It was in Valencia that he began to get

> a sense of the place, because, growing up otherwise in Port of Spain, you didn't see bele, you didn't know nothing about bongo, you didn't know nothing about fine play – all the things that I later came to know and to appreciate, hadn't been exposed to me before. But once I got there and began to see it, I began to understand what we have and where things came from. That was the beginning of a kind of search and research into the culture that we have. (Personal interview, April 2010)

Lovelace worked as a field assistant (forest ranger) in the Department of Forestry from 1954 to 1956. He was based in the rural village of Valencia (on the road to Toco, his birthplace) in the eastern part of Trinidad. Although his maternal grandfather had worked his plot of land in Fort George, Scarborough, Tobago, he had been excluded from farm work on health grounds. His posting to Valencia as a forest ranger was, therefore, his first real opportunity to get to know the land and those who lived on, and off, it.

In Port of Spain, although he had started to create a circle of friends drawn from the staff of the *Guardian* and some old school friends with whom he played football, table tennis and cricket and went to fetes, he never really got to know people beyond their function-specific friendships: football friends, table tennis friends, cricket friends. When he arrived in Valencia, he realized that he was a stranger, an outsider, a civil servant with no vested interest in the community, no history to influence people's initial judgement of him, and with no family loyalties to cloud his own responses to any of the villagers or theirs to him. Ironically, however, it was this outsider status in Valencia that would make him acceptable to many of the villagers and invest him with the freedom and open-mindedness to know the people, their landscape and their world view:

> I went to Valencia as a Forest Ranger, knowing nothing of the forest, nothing really of rural Trinidad. The place was bush, all around was forest. The houses were almost all carat roofed. The people were ordinary, principally unlettered people, but they were the most beautiful people I would get to know. I went on the truck with them and up in the forest. As someone unaccustomed to the forest, I would be thirsty. They knew what vines to cut to get water and I suppose they were delighted to have someone to show their world to. There were people who went hunting for wild beast. I went a couple times, but I didn't like hunting. Didn't like to see the animals hunted and killed. (Lovelace, AIP)

CHAPTER TWO

The job with the *Guardian* had put him in direct contact with words, the primary tools of writers. The job in Valencia was an equally ideal job for a writer, especially one who was in search of a community and a vision. In Valencia, Lovelace developed the practice of full participation in communal activities, although he "kept a private space for reading, for scribbling, for thinking". Before Valencia, he had begun to nurse the desire to write but he did not know what and who to write about. Valencia provided him with the opportunity of "finding and consolidating the vantage point of community from which I would view the world" (Lovelace, AIP). The impact of the knowledge of community that he developed in Valencia was critical to his ability to conceptualize and write his first novel, *While Gods Are Falling*:

> After I had settled in Valencia, I felt free to decide what I really wanted to do. . . . There was one thing that I felt I could do that was important and that was to write. I had been scribbling for some time, little things, unfinished, unclear, that I had shown to no one, that belonged to my secret space. . . . There was not a library in the village, but the public library van came every Thursday and I had begun to borrow books from it. Writing was what I had been preparing myself for, even though I didn't quite know it. It was what I thought would satisfy me, even more than sports which I was pretty good at though not outstanding, not only because of lack of talent but because I could never bring myself to make that supreme effort which I believe is what is required to be a good athlete, the ability to make, with consistency, that supreme effort, to play consistently at your best. . . . I knew I would write anyway, so I decided to

> put my real effort into writing. . . . I had, I should say, never even seen a real writer nor met one.
>
> Once I made the decision, I decided that I would . . . read every day even if it was one page and write every day even if it was a line. I would also need to educate myself. . . . And for many years, I did just that – read and wrote every day. I began to read books on philosophy, psychology, history and of course books of fiction. (Lovelace, AIP)

Valencia was where Lovelace's future as a writer began to take shape, both in his mind and on paper. One of the results of his earliest attempts at writing is the unpublished, handwritten "A Manicou Hunt".[11] The story is based on a hunting trip he had taken with a woodsman into the Valencia forest. Valencia provided him with a community whose stories and aspirations could form the contents of his work. But he still had to find the way to write them and the vision with which to illuminate them:

> When I began to write seriously, I discovered that my sentences were not complete, that I hadn't said completely what I wanted to say and I thought that I could never be a writer because I thought that writers wrote fluently from beginning to end, then I found a book in the library on writing fiction and it talked about revision, that writing was like a bit of sculpture, that you could shape it until you got what you wanted. To say that that advice helped will be an understatement, it saved me. (Lovelace, AIP)

Lovelace might have found the landscape and the characters for his fiction in rural areas, among the ordinary people of Valencia and, later, the other rural communities where the government was a distant echo, but he also recognized, from very early, starting with his time in school in Port of Spain and at work at the *Guardian*, the importance of Port of Spain as the socio-political and economic centre of the nation. This understanding of the interlocking destinies of the rural and the urban is self-evident in *While Gods Are Falling*, *The Dragon Can't Dance*, *Salt* and *Is Just a Movie*. Consciously or unconsciously, Port of Spain had taken as deep-seated a hold on his imagination as the rural areas that he had consciously embraced. When he lived in Valencia, he made regular forays into Port of Spain and its environs to attend literary events and to listen to Eric Williams's galvanizing speeches about history, identity, liberation and independence at Woodford Square in Port of Spain, which had been proclaimed the University of Woodford Square by the masses in recognition of the intense and revolutionary political education that was taking place there. When the People's National Movement eventually rolled out to Valencia, Lovelace was one of those who "went immediately and signed up to become members of the [People's National Movement] party" (Lovelace, AIP). He does not think that he ever received the party card since they might have forgotten to include the necessary registration fees with the application forms they sent to the party headquarters (private conversation).

No sooner did he begin to settle into, and to embrace and be embraced by, Valencia than he was set to move on. A colleague in forestry had drawn his attention to an opening in the agricultural department, and, because agriculture was more glamorous than forestry and the job came with a motor bike, Lovelace had applied. He was interviewed, selected, and, after a three-month orientation at the St Joseph Farm, posted to the Demonstration Station, Rio Claro, as the field assistant in charge of the station.

In 1956, Rio Claro was much bigger than Valencia but it was, nonetheless, also significantly rural. It was "a town with a Catholic church and an Anglican church, an Adventist church and Sweet Papa – an Orisha leader with a Shango palais, a court house and police station, post office but not a library, a scale house for weighing canes and a buying house where farmers brought cocoa beans. It was the agricultural centre for the areas around Biche, Cushe, Mayaro" (Lovelace, AIP).

The years he spent in Rio Claro provided Lovelace with the opportunity to deepen his understanding of rural communities and, because of the more pronounced ethnic mix, especially of Africans and Indians, of the multicultural impulse in the psyche of the country. Rio Claro, a town that had also featured in his mother's journeys through Trinidad, would become a special place in Lovelace's development as a poet, novelist, playwright and husband.

After three years in Rio Claro, he went to the Eastern Caribbean Institute of Agriculture and Forestry, Centeno (then known as the Eastern Caribbean Farm Institute) to study for a diploma in forestry. In the three years in Rio Claro before leaving for Centeno, he had joined other mid-level civil servants and teachers to play cricket and football. Outside of the cricket and football, he spent time in the gambling club where he interacted with the ordinary people of the town, including some of its notorious badjohns who, in addition to those he had known or known of in Port of Spain and Valencia, would subsequently be transformed into major protagonists in his fiction, ranging from Bolo in *The Wine of Astonishment*, through Fisheye in *The Dragon Can't Dance*, to Sonnyboy in *Is Just a Movie*, operating as metaphors of an instinctive, albeit sometimes misguided or not fully rationalized or orchestrated, rebellion against oppression and exploitation.

If Valencia and Rio Claro provided the landscape and manscape of Trinidad that would inform Lovelace's writing, his two years at the Eastern Caribbean Farm Institute, Centeno provided the stage for his understanding of the inter-island dynamics of the Caribbean, an awareness of the significance of sports in forming communal spirit, and the discovery of his own personal leadership potential and mettle. The school also provided him with the platform to try out his writing on a captive but barely interested audience and to discover that he would need to be single-minded and focused if he was serious about becoming a writer in a world that cared very little for literature:

> ECFI [Eastern Caribbean Farm Institute] was my first tertiary institution. There we learned about agriculture, we each had a plot on which we planted things and tried out pesticides and fertilisers, milked cows, tended crops and got a good sense of what was useful for farming. We lived together, fellars from the Eastern Caribbean and Guyana. . . . We played in a cricket league and we played football in an Arima league, we had sports

> meetings, we had fetes for carnival, we were out there in the lonely world of Centeno. . . . But it was good living together, getting to know each other, to match yourself against fellows your age, you discovered who you were in this milieu. I discovered myself as a leader and came to represent fellows, not officially. I felt a certain impatience at not being elsewhere, thinking about writing and having to study, to get up and get to practical on time after spending most of the night writing and reading. It was a nervous time. I suppose I was one of the rebels. (Lovelace, AIP)

It was here that Lovelace took another concrete step towards realizing his dream of becoming a writer. He bought himself a typewriter for twenty-seven dollars and began to write:

> I was writing then and when fellars were relaxing playing cards, I would go into the room, sit on the floor and while the game was going on would begin to read. They cussed me. They called me mad. They ridiculed me. I kept on. I had to endure their cussing, their wanting to chase me out the room, their laughter, their certainty that I was a mad man. I would just go on reading and if the story held them, one might laugh at something or comment. I would get an idea of how successful the story was or what needed work. But they were not alone in their alarm over my preoccupation with writing. Once, my brother Talbot came to see me and I was anxious to show him the place, to show him my room and what I was writing. I noticed him looking at me with some reserve, nodding his head and saying, yes yes, yes. Later I learned that he went to my sister Lyris and said to her, "I think Earl going mad." So I was the Mad Man at ECFI. (Lovelace, AIP)

CHAPTER TWO

His description of his relationship with his audience at the Eastern Caribbean Farm Institute is so different from what it has become in his years as a successful writer. His readings are now highly anticipated. Audiences at home and abroad are enchanted by his breathless prose, his narrative foreplays and hold-backs, and his well-primed humour.

The annual magazine of the Eastern Caribbean Farm Institute, the *Frog Hopper*, 1962 edition, has preserved the personality of Lovelace, the emerging writer. The magazine was the platform for his first public outing as a writer and as an editor. His first known published works are in that maiden issue of the *Frog Hopper*. He contributed the editorial, poetry and fiction to the issue. With the benefit of hindsight, his contributions contained the seeds of many of his subsequent major artistic and ideological, if not stylistic, preoccupations as a writer.

In addition to his editorial and literary contributions to this magazine, there are a number of pen-portraits of him by his classmates, with information that can be deconstructed to yield insights into the kind of writer and person he has become.

This issue of the *Frog Hopper* establishes four key characteristics of the young Lovelace: (1) although he was in training as an agricultural assistant, his passion was for writing; (2) he was preoccupied with the concept of nation-building, especially as it related to the relationship between the individual and the community; (3) he was both an aspiring short-story writer and a poet; and (4) he was an accomplished athlete, excelling in cricket (at some point in his cricketing "career", his cricket sobriquet was Mezzo), football, athletics and table tennis.

In the editorial, Lovelace underscores the need for citizen-participation in the development of community:

> To my mind, living and participation are very closely bound up, simply because participation more often than not involves co-operation, one of the most, if not the most necessary ingredient in society. . . . We might say that he who is willing to participate is also willing to cooperate. Dancing, talking, playing are some expressions of participation. Undertaken together they help to draw us closer together and aid in the expansion of interests which mankind have in common. (*Frog Hopper*, May 1962, 5)

Lovelace would further develop the concept of citizen-participation as a central philosophical plank both in his fiction and in his polemical essays.[12] Similarly, the tragedy of Ivan Morton in *The Wine of Astonishment* is triggered by his betrayal of his enabling community and his embrace of the hegemonic tradition of the colonizers. In *The Dragon Can't Dance*, on the other hand, we see how social responsibility without the prerequisite philosophical base can be self-defeating. But in *Salt*, Lovelace articulates the possibilities for success inherent in the collaboration between native intellectuals and educated intellectuals (Bango and Alford), as well as between races and classes. In essence, the need for members of a community to have a say in the governance of the community has remained a consistent aspect of Lovelace's model for social re-engineering. That principle informs Bango's demand for reparation that recognizes the pain of victims and victimizers alike, as well as teacher Alford George's epiphany, which concedes leadership to the ordinary people led by Bango and his wife, marching side by side. It is the same desire for participation that propelled the Gang of Nine to launch into their impulsive march for change in *The Dragon Can't Dance*. However, in both novels, Lovelace is quick to signify that there are other ingredients (a properly articulated philosophy and a plan of action – complete with contingency plans) that are required to make citizen-participation effective. Fisheye and his team fail mainly because they had neither a body of ideas nor a coherent plan of action to guide their anger. It is only during their incarceration that they begin to discuss the need for philosophical and ideological imperatives. Bango, on the other hand, is anchored by the ancestral philosophy and narratives embedded in his history. He deploys the lessons learned from that history to refine his responses to his contemporary context. He does this so well and honestly that some of his most belligerent critics, like his wife, would eventually come around to his vision of life and stand with him, shoulder to shoulder, at the critical moment, to memorialize his ideas of freedom and to force the political elites to listen to his demand for reparation and self-reliance.

Another key issue raised by Lovelace in his editorial was that "dancing, talking, playing are some expressions of participation. Undertaken together, they help to draw us closer together and aid in the expansion of interests which mankind have in common" (*Frog Hopper*, May 1962, 5). The art of playing has remained very central to Lovelace's world and work, fictional or otherwise. Lovelace loves to dance. He sees dance as an essential mode for both personal and group communication. He loves life and a good lime; he is famous for his infectious deep-throated I-am-alive laughter; he is not averse to playing wappie (a card game, often played for money) now and again; he loves to talk his ideas through with others; and he is famous for testing out his work-in-progress through public readings (a carry-over of his practice at the Eastern Caribbean Farm Institute where he would, without their approval, read his work to his schoolmates, who, not surprisingly, eventually characterized him as the "crazy philosopher", a "mental wreck", and "Ogden" after the poetry-spouting, sometimes villainous, buffoon from the cartoon strip, *Dick Tracy*).[13]

The referencing of dance in the editorial may be generic, but his experiences in rural communities would further expose him to specialized dances and musical traditions like the bongo (funeral wake), parang and stick-fighting kalinda, all of which would reveal to him the different layers of the indigenous responses to history, and out of which he would construct complex metaphors of the postcolonial state of the region. In *The Dragon Can't Dance*, the metaphor of dance functions both as a trope of postcolonial cultural possibilities, especially in the context of carnival, and as a metaphor for the balancing/mesmerizing acts of political contestations in post-independence Trinidad and Tobago. Like two stickfighters locked in mortal combat, each displaying his or her dancing skills and fancy footwork before moving in for the blow, the Gang of Nine and the political establishment dance around each other, each one looking for an opening to deliver a victory blow. The fighter who is agile, adaptive, quick-footed and able to think on his or her feet wins in the end. In this dance of violence, the Gang of Nine is defeated in the end because it lacks a philosophical foundation for its revolt/dance and has no countermove to the prime minister's master stroke of directing that all gas stations should be closed, thus ensuring that the gang could not refuel the police jeep it had commandeered and was driving around to deliver their call to action to the public.

In *The Dragon Can't Dance*, dance is also presented as a palliative, a cure-all for the pains of dispossession and political exploitation. Dance is Calvary Hill's carnival answer to the frustrations of life, the affirmation of the women's sexuality and their spirituality, and a marker of the children's aliveness.

But it is not only at the political level that Lovelace has deployed the metaphor of dance for the articulation of his social philosophy. In the short story "Call Me 'Miss Ross' For Now" (*Brief Conversion*, 65), dance/fete is juxtaposed with a village council meeting, with the village council representing a preoccupation with the political and the dance a place for the non-verbal negotiation of desires and the actualization of the personal and the emotional. At the beginning of the story, forty-seven-year-old Miss Ross is too conservative to take advantage of her sexuality and too traditional to be seen at a dance without a man. But by the end of the story, she is running away from the village council meeting, presumably to go to a dance, with her girlfriend and with no man between them, but with the hope of finding one there.

Lovelace's best theorizing of dance is to be found in some of his essays in *Growing in the Dark*. He insists that in order to fully apprehend the history of the New World African, one must take into account the metalanguage of the folk culture, especially dance. He argues that while the African may not have had a wealth of written history, he has an alternative source of history as contained in his dances and songs and stories:

> These songs, dances, and stories, I want to suggest are a living source of our authentic history. When we look at our dances and listen to our songs, when we experience the vitality and power of the steelband and hear a stickfight chant and watch the leaps and dexterity of the bongo dance and the self-affirmation and sauciness of bele or the brisk affirming energy of the pique, we know we have a history of ourselves as subjects. It has not been erased, for it is carried in our bodies.[14]

In a 1987 essay, "Caribbean Folk Culture within the Process of Modernisation", he argues that dancing "is perhaps the most affirmative human expression of self, indicating as it does, the exercise by the individual of power/control over his own body".[15] In "The Ongoing Value of Our Indigenous Traditions",[16] he asserts that "the body became an instrument over which the [African] had control. And if you look at African dances you will see that they show the body in control of itself. The dancer is not seeking to traverse space, like the waltz and other European dances, but concentrates on mastering his/her body within a limited space. The body becomes the universe."[17] And more recently, he has refined dance into a signifier of the tension between colonial and postcolonial attitudes to freedom:

> I don't know how many of you have ever lined up to get into a dance, where you are not certain of your welcome. Where, at the door, there is some kind of restriction, maybe it is the dress code, or your colour, or your class, or you don't know the people and they don't know you and all your energies are focused on getting past that door. And you fix your dress and you fix your smile and you try to calm yourself and eventually you get in. . . . And when you get in, it is as if you have carried the uncertainties with you, you can't really leggo, you feel inhibited, you feel you must behave in a certain way, you feel you must restrict your behaviour to what you believe that they would expect of you. You go to move, the way you want to move, and you believe somebody is watching you. . . . You in the dance, but you acting as if you owe the people you meet there something, you acting as if they somehow have more rights than you. And so you will behave in accordance with how they behave. . . . That, I want to suggest to you is the colonial perspective, restricted to what he has had to overcome in order to get into the dance. . . . There is another fellow who has the same experience at the door and his response is to continue to wave his credentials, his ticket, the way some people wave their degrees, and continues to be preoccupied with his hair, his tie and jacket and with upholding what he thinks to be the rules and restrictions of the fete. He cannot ever cut loose. . . . You on the other hand have had no trouble at the door, you are inside the dance and your job is to dance. You have the self-confidence and we hope, the moves; and, if you don't have them, you have to get them, you have to learn them. The dance is yours. You have to take over the fete.[18]

It is clear from the above that Lovelace has refined the metaphor of dance into complex permutations capable of articulating a range of historical as well as contemporary imperatives and possibilities.

The self-confidence needed to take charge of the dance underscores one of his two poems in the *Frog Hopper* (May 1962, 32). In "Independence: The West Indies", he imagines West Indian independence as a new home with an owner who is either "not ready to be boss" or full of reckless abandon, "creating havoc in the very house / You must soon possess". This theme will resurface in his 1962 play *The New Boss*, a play about an estate that has been left by the owners for their African and Indian workers. "Sunset", the other poem in the magazine, examines the concept of the cycle of life. This poem signals Lovelace's engagement and fascination with nature, which will find deeper articulation in *The Schoolmaster*, where he deploys pathetic fallacy for aesthetic, philosophical and thematic amplification.

Although Lovelace would go on to write some more poems, he would not become a major poetic voice. Instead, he would channel his poetic talent into songwriting for his plays, calypsoes and the occasional poems in his fiction (especially in *Salt*, *The Dragon Can't Dance* and the short story "Joebell in America"). He even flirted with the idea of becoming a calypsonian, adopting the sobriquet of Lord Farmer, a name given to him by the calypsonian Lord Blakie (private conversation).

There is only one tangential reference to dance in "Fools", his short story in the *Frog Hopper*, but the reference establishes dance as a standard preoccupation of the community of students in the story. "Fools" contains intimations of ideas that would become central in Lovelace's writing. It presents a conflict between two roommates from two Caribbean nations (Trinidad and Barbados), both of whom deploy the negative stereotypical concepts they have of each other against each other. Interestingly enough, on the surface, Lovelace's literary canvas has shrunk from the regional reach in "Fools" to a national gaze in his novels and plays, as he moves to validate his credo that "nobody is born into the world. Every one of us is born into a place in the world, in a culture, and it is from that standpoint of culture that we contribute to the world."[19] However, a more discerning exploration of his work will reveal that regionalism has remained a concern in his work. While the primary gaze in *Salt* is the enterprise of Trinidad and Tobago, from colonialism through independence to post-colonialism, it opens with a description of a political evolution that acknowledges the pan-Caribbean spectrum inherent in its bedrock: "But these fellars here. These fellars was the most lawless and rebellious set of fellars they had in the Caribbean, the majority of them dangerous rebels exiled here from the other islands, men that have no cure, fellars whose sport is to bust one another head, fellars who make up their mind to dead, who land from Martinique and Grenada and St Lucia and from wherever they bring them" (*Salt*, 6).

"Fools" ends with a carnivalesque scene, foreshadowing the band at the end of *The Wine of Astonishment*, the Bangoled marchers at the end of *Salt*, and the jouvay/old mas surrealistic atmosphere that rounds off *Is Just a Movie*. The collectivized response with which Lovelace closes "Fools" will go through several iterations to emerge as an organically evolved denouement in *Salt* and *Is Just a Movie*.

On the evidence of the pen-portraits in the *Frog Hopper*, the young Lovelace was a notable cricketer, excelling in bowling; an experienced, confident and exciting-to-watch table tennis player (when in form); and an athlete and a good tackler at centre-half in football but given to excessive dribbling and quick to anger. These athletic exploits would inform his characterization of Alford as an aspiring cricketer turned umpire; Carabon, whose integration is made possible because of his exploits on the football field (*Salt*); and Franklyn as a legendary batsman in *Is Just a Movie*. In all of these instances, Lovelace presents sport as an identity former, a character builder and a bridge-builder in a multicultural society. The arrival at this vision would have been inspired by his own participation in sports at school, in Valencia, Rio Claro and, especially, at the Eastern Caribbean Farm Institute, where sports facilitated the bonding among students in his class who came from all over the region (twelve from Trinidad and Tobago, three from Barbados, seven from British Guiana [Guyana], one from Antigua, one from St Kitts, one from Montserrat, two from Dominica, two from Grenada, one from St Vincent, and two from St Lucia in his year) to create a community at Centeno. Today, outside of the University of the West Indies and, maybe, CARICOM, cricket is one area in which the region has not completely succumbed to insularity.

CHAPTER TWO

Lovelace's performance in one of the subjects for the diploma in forestry was below par and earned him a referral in the subject. He had to be re-examined in that subject the following year (1963) before he could be awarded his diploma. The referral cost him his place in the order of seniority in the civil service. Instead of moving up in the system in 1962, after his stint at Centeno, he was re-posted to his original position in Rio Claro for what would turn out to be the second of three stints there. Naturally, he was upset about the referral. He had completed arrangements to go to the Sir George Williams University in Canada to study but his referral torpedoed his plan. He was also unhappy that he had been re-posted to Rio Claro. This was like a public confirmation of the professional stagnation in his life.

The Rio Claro he returned to had not changed physically but there was a different spirit in the air. The cricket and football clubs he had played with were now defunct as most of the members had gone abroad to study. He joined the Penetrators, a football team that was made up of mainly unemployed and barely employed young men. The composition of the Penetrators was a far cry from the clubs he had played with before he went to Centeno, which were made up of teachers and civil servants.

The Centeno experience had confirmed, for Lovelace, the need for, and possibility of, a collective regional spirit, but with the collapse of the West Indies Federation, the independence of the individual islands was the next best option. So invested was Lovelace in the spirit of the impending independence that he submitted lyrics for the competition for the national anthem of Trinidad and Tobago. He was in Port of Spain to see the flag raised and to listen to the speech by the prime minister, Dr Eric Williams. He wrote an independence play, *The New Boss*, which he directed using the players from the Penetrators football team. It played on an open-air stage on the grounds of the Shell Oil Company in Rio Claro. These players-turned-actors became the friends with whom he spent time discussing the politics of the newly independent nation, with him as their guide. Their stories, their search for enlightenment, and their struggle for a place in the world would eventually populate many of the short stories in *A Brief Conversion*.

Up until his return to Rio Claro in 1962, most of Lovelace's romantic interests were perfunctory, short-lived and strictly about negotiating sex. His preference was for casual dalliances. Among his visitors in Valencia

> were two young women who came in the night, one came in the night and left later. The other lived next door. I don't know and I never asked how she did it, but she would leave her house and appear in my room and would remain the entire night and then leave before dawn. What is remarkable was that these liaisons were strictly about sex, we didn't talk very much and I didn't have any great feelings towards them. It is only after it was over for whatever reason that I felt how I had missed out on loving them. (Lovelace, AIP)

But on his return to Rio Claro, his attitude to relationships would change significantly as a result of his meeting an Indo-

CHAPTER TWO

Trinidadian schoolteacher, Jean Gadjadhar, and the fact of their falling in love. One narrative has it that his eventual posting out of Rio Claro to Tobago had something to do with Jean's father, who worked in the same ministry as Lovelace and disapproved of his daughter's interracial relationship. He is alleged to have pulled a few strings to get Lovelace transferred to Tobago with the hope that the distance would put a damper on the relationship. Another version of the story claims that the choice of who went to Tobago was between Lovelace and another colleague, and that because the colleague was married with children and Lovelace was a bachelor, the lot fell on Lovelace.

At some point before his posting to Tobago, a friend (Pricilla Moses) brought a newspaper clipping announcing the BP Independence Literary Award to him, with the hope that he would submit his work for the competition. The prize was to be awarded to a manuscript of a novel written about Trinidad and Tobago by a hitherto unpublished citizen. Lovelace was at that point busy putting together a collection of his poems for possible publication. He promptly put aside the poems, took out a novel he had been working on and finished writing it a day before the deadline for submission. He left for Tobago soon after submitting the manuscript.

After two days in Tobago, Lovelace was back in Trinidad.

He took a taxi to the school where Jean was teaching in Mayaro and proposed to her. She asked him to speak to her mother, which he did. Her mother asked him to speak to Jean's father. But, knowing that her father was opposed to their relationship, Lovelace refused. Nonetheless, Jean agreed to marry him.

The wedding was set for the Anglican church in Rio Claro and was almost like something straight out of a Lovelace fiction or, more correctly, something that fed into his fiction:

> It was a small affair with my sister [Lyris] coming from Port of Spain and my friends from Rio Claro. The plan was that my good friend Cecil would be best man. But he had problems with transport. I intuited that something was wrong and I went to the junction to see if I could find one of the fellars to deputise for him. I saw Figgy and asked him to go and change and come with me to the church. Jean had none of her family there. . . . We got married and next couple days we set out for Tobago. (Lovelace, AIP)

In Tobago, Lovelace became friends with the artist and cultural anthropologist Eddie Hernandez (he would direct the Tobago premiere of The New Boss in 1964) and his young protégé, Jim Armstrong, and he began the process of re-familiarizing himself with the landscape of his childhood memories. As he had done in Valencia and in Rio Claro, he joined football and cricket groups in Scarborough. He was also constantly thinking of the BP Independence Literary Award and affirming to Jean that he was going to win it, if only because of the originality of the title of his manuscript. When he was informed that his entry had been shortlisted by the local judging team of John Makin (the British Council representative in Trinidad) and Errol Hill (staff tutor in creative arts for the Extra-Mural Department of the University of the West Indies) to be adjudicated on by the British writer J.B. Priestley, he became even more convinced that he was destined to win. And he did, becoming five thousand dollars richer.

It was befitting that the act of winning his first literary prize should happen while he was in Tobago, the place where he had started his lifelong love of reading. *While Gods Are Falling* won from an impressive field of thirty-two entries that included, as finalists, *The Obeah Man* by Ismith Khan, *The Dry Season* by Isaac Boodhoo and *Pan Beat* by Marion Glean.

The win changed Lovelace's life dramatically. On the subsequent evidence of his relationship with poetry, his success in the competition seemed to have inspired him to concentrate on prose fiction. While the quality of his published and unpublished poems is admirable, the quality of his fiction is by far superior to that of his poetry. He wrote two fiction manuscripts in quick succession after *While Gods Are Falling*.[20] Although they were never published, many of the issues raised in them – such as the role of education and sports in identity formation; obsession with emigration, race, and class relations; historical links between the New World and Africa/India; and the emergence of the Eric Williams phenomenon – have remained central issues in his works.

The BP Independence Literary Award established Lovelace as a writer. He made headlines not as a forest ranger, not as an agricultural assistant, not as a sport personality but as a prize-winning writer. Eric Roach, one of the leading poets in the country, went to Tobago to interview him for the *Guardian* newspaper (*Sunday Guardian*, 26 July 1964) and reviewed the book when it was eventually published in 1965. J.B. Priestley visited Trinidad to present Lovelace with the prize at a ceremony at Hilton Hotel and visited Tobago with his wife to have lunch with Earl and Jean.

The full import of the BP Independence Literary Award became even more evident when the book was published in 1965 to modest reviews. C.L.R. James celebrated Lovelace in the company of Michael Anthony as examples of "native writers" who were advancing "our sense of national identity" (*People*, 25 June 1965). In November 1965, he was honoured for his contribution to literature with the Pegasus Literary Award alongside Slinger Francisco (the Mighty Sparrow) for music, Julia Edwards for dance, Alf Codallo for cultural research, Ken Morris for art and Errol Hill for theatre.

Another implication of the prize was the fact that, finally, Lovelace had money to go away to study. He opted for the United States (Howard University in Washington, DC) over England. His choice was informed by his desire to move away from the so-called Mother Country. His choice of Howard might have been, in part, informed by the significance of that institution in the political trajectory of Eric Williams, whose lectures on the history and people of Trinidad and Tobago had struck a chord with the young Lovelace.

Before leaving for the United States, he had started to write *The Schoolmaster* and wanted to talk with his grandfather to find out from him what he knew about the spirit world and the experience of enslavement in Tobago. But the most he got out of him was how he used to own horses and nearly horsewhipped a white man over one of the horses. That story inspired the character of Benn in *The Schoolmaster*.

CHAPTER TWO

He left for Howard University in 1966 with the hope of specializing either in sociology or literature. But, at the end of the first year, he decided to return home because he felt that the Howard education he was being exposed to was not what he wanted: "It wasn't what I thought it would be. I thought that I would come to learn but I wasn't learning. . . . I didn't see it happening. I saw it really as a certification rather than a centre of learning and I was brave enough then to say, 'No, I ain't able with this.' So I left" (personal interview, 1995).

But there was also another source of frustration for Lovelace. He had gone up to Howard alone, ahead of Jean and their first child, Walt. On his own, it was easy to survive on the barest minimum, but when Jean and Walt joined him, their arrival complicated his financial situation. With money running out and without a job, the family decided to return to Trinidad. In an interview with Carl Jacobs of the *Sunday Guardian* (8 October 1967, 9), Lovelace added a third reason for his return: he did not find the time to write as he had wanted. This is, of course, not surprising, since he had invested a lot of his time in the civil rights activities on the campus. That involvement would, however, help to consolidate his evolving consciousness of struggle and justice, which experience would serve him well on his return to Trinidad and Tobago at a time when the Black Power movement was beginning to emerge.

Inevitably, he also came up against American racism while in the United States. His first personal experience of American racism happened in the summer of 1966. He had a job teaching writing in the Upward Bound Program at Virginia Union College. One day, he set out to buy bread across the road from the campus. A white female colleague offered to go with him. As they waited for the light to change for them to cross the road, he noticed that an open-top car with four white men had stopped and the driver was honking at them. It took him a while to realize that he was the subject of their anger and that his crime was that he was with a white girl. If he had any doubt about the need for the Civil Rights Movement and for Black Power, that episode erased such doubts. He never went anywhere with her after that experience.

In a future to come (1971) and also in Washington, DC, he would be at the receiving end of another form of American racism – police profiling of black men. Gregory Rigsby, his friend from the Howard years, relates:

> The occasion was when a slight drizzle began to fall. Earl, "like back home", as he explained it, began to run for shelter. Well, about six police squad cars, with lights flashing and sirens blaring, surrounded him within a few minutes. He didn't then know that a black man couldn't run on a street in DC without being suspected of a crime. "The policemen did not even apologise self. They just say that I fitted the description of someone they were looking for." After a reflexive pause, he added, "These people up here wicked, you hear." Next day, rumour has it that, as someone went to pick him up to go on an assignment, he saw Earl walking up and down the sidewalk. "Why you walking like that, man?" Earl pointed to a sign that said "No Standing", and after the previous day's experience with the police, he didn't want to have "to deal with these DC police". Of course, the "No

Standing" sign applied to vehicles. But Earl had tasted the DC police officers of the early 1970s.[21]

The return of Lovelace to Trinidad and Tobago in 1967 coincided with the establishment of the *Express* newspaper as the first post-independence, indigenously owned newspaper in the country. According to a report in the *Express* of 14 October 1967, Lovelace was so excited about "what the *Express* has to offer, that as soon as he had settled down and unpacked his bags last week, he made a bee-line for Express House". With his one year of college experience, his prize-winning novel and the manuscript of his soon-to-be-published *The Schoolmaster* to recommend him, Lovelace was offered a job in the editorial department of the *Express*.

The political changes he had witnessed and in which he had participated in the United States had filtered into Trinidad and Tobago. The *Express* and its writers would bear witness to, and reflect on, these changes as they evolved. Woodford Square, also known as the University of Woodford Square, which had been the central venue for the lectures of Eric Williams in the late 1950s, was renamed the People's Parliament and taken over by radical ideologues and native intellectuals, from where they launched their analyses of the failures of the government of Eric Williams. Experimental artists and poets were creating new forms, especially performance poetry with drum accompaniment, to express their discontent; political analysts were searching for independent theories to make sense of the politics; and radical workers' unions were espousing socialist visions.

In his inaugural piece for the *Express* (15 October 1967, 8), Lovelace confessed that he did not see himself "in the role of either knight in shining armour or martyr". His rejection of the role of messiah, he argued, was informed by his reading of the character of the nation as one in which people were only too willing to "designate 'exceptional' individuals and then leave things up to them, and withdraw into their own comfortable corners" from where they could "criticise in articulate whispers, secure in the feeling that no blame or responsibility for the chaos that would result from such circumstances could attach itself to them". He rejected the option of despair, abdication of responsibility or exile and, instead, recommended collective involvement in the process of "building a country that we can respect and where we are respected, a country in which one's humanity means something". Although these comments were coming on the heels of his American experience, which had caused him to "reflect on our shallow middleclassness which is both stultifying and inhibiting", it is also true that he has always been concerned about the need for collective involvement and the need to locate humanity at the centre of development. Later in his career, in an interview with Ronald John of the *Trinidad Guardian* (26 August 1987), while assessing the implications of his location in Trinidad and Tobago, Lovelace would state: "My advantage over writers who have migrated is that I am more acutely aware of what is taking place here now. This enables me to address myself to themes in this society with much more confidence and depth; to present a Caribbean perspective on the world; advance our language and sensibility, undermining and destroying those negative images . . . self-imposed upon us by a view of history, which has hitherto presented us as objects."

The *Express* gave Lovelace a platform to reflect on the Black Power revolution, both as an observer and as a participant. This involvement was particularly instrumental in initiating a new trajectory in the thematic concerns in his work. It enabled him to refine his presentation of the African dimension of the multicultural character of Trinidad and Tobago. In his first two novels, written before the time of Black Power, while it was possible to intuit the ethnicities of the characters, their presentation is basically generic, associated more with class and professions than with race. But in *The Wine of Astonishment*, his gaze is decidedly African, presented through the prism of the official suppression of the Africa-inspired Spiritual Baptist faith. He saw the writing of this novel as part of the process of uncovering the history of the place, of beginning to "see ourselves as more than having a history of slavery and colonialism but as having a history which I would write later as a history of a struggle against enslavement, indenture, and colonialism, as belonging to something more and that we were in the process of reclaiming ourselves" (*Caribbean Contact*, June 1977, 15). For a writer who had been politically conscious from childhood and one writing out of a multicultural region like the Caribbean, it is intriguing that the issue of race as a major factor in the social engineering of the society could be absent from his first two published novels. Lovelace admits that *The Wine of Astonishment* is

> the first novel in which I decided to be black . . . I wanted to make a definite statement. I think I wanted to establish the character's blackness, establish where they came from. If you look at *The Schoolmaster* you will see that although one was able to identify people, there is no colour at all. You will not find the word "black" although one gets the impression while reading it that one is talking about black people. The word "white" is used once with reference to the priest. (Ibid.)

The same is true of *While Gods Are Falling* in which class tensions predominate.

Why is race absent from his first two novels? Was it that race was not such an important issue in the Tobago of his childhood, an island that is almost homogenously African? Caught in the heady dreams of the nationalism that accompanied independence, was an idealistic Lovelace so consumed with the promise of independence that he preferred to sublimate the divisive issue of race? Was it that his life in rural Trinidad had demonstrated and convinced him that most citizens of the countryside placed little emphasis on race? Lovelace was, of course, not untouched by the contestations consequent on the cross-cultural dynamics of Trinidad, if not Tobago. He was himself subjected to these tensions when his prospective Indian father-in-law objected to his relationship with his daughter, an event that happened before he finished writing his first novel. Whatever may be the right question, answer or surmising, Lovelace's choice of primarily African settings for his first two novels precluded the centrality of multiculturalism and the attendant complications of race relations.

CHAPTER TWO

While Gods Are Falling is set in a tenement building on the edge of Port of Spain during a period that roughly approximates the early stages of independence. Lovelace would return to this landscape and history with more discerning eyes in *The Dragon Can't Dance*, at a time in history (1970) when the African/Indian contestations would have become impossible to ignore.

While Gods Are Falling belongs to the sub-genre of yard literature, even though the notion of Webber Street, its setting as a yard, is not explicitly articulated. Webber Street anticipates the more obviously yardish Calvary Hill in *The Dragon Can't Dance*. In addition to the signature Lovelace thematic concerns in *While Gods Are Falling*, the stylistic experiments in it are precursors of his style in his mature fiction. The folkloric/vernacular/folksy tone at the beginning of the book would be taken to a new level in *The Dragon Can't Dance*, *The Wine of Astonishment* and, at an even more refined level, *Salt*. The presentation of Webber Street as a faceless, nameless throng of humanity succeeds in reinforcing the official erasure of the masses, but it does not evoke the complexity of the space in the same way as his subsequent novels where setting is not just incidental but integrative. Similarly, his deployment of given names and descriptor names (Walter Castle/bandy-legged one or Mr Cross/one-legged) would be refined in *The Dragon Can't Dance* to narratively carry the burden of the struggle between the real-selves and the role/stage-selves of the characters, as in the parallel between Aldrick (real-self) and the Dragon (role/stage-self) or Belasco (real-self) and Fisheye (role/stage-self).

In 1968, Lovelace left the *Express* (as a regular member of staff) and Port of Spain to return to Rio Claro for the third time. His relocation was to enable him to "pursue writing as a full-time occupation. More specifically, to write this book that I had in mind" (personal interview, June 1995). But life stalled that plan and the book, *The Wine of Astonishment*, would not be published until 1982.

As soon as he arrived in Rio Claro, Lovelace got caught up in the life of the town, taking a lead role in organizing the community to respond to the revolutionary events that were taking shape in the country and which would culminate in the 1970 uprisings against the government of Eric Williams. So visibly involved was he (he had plastered his Volkswagen car with Black Power slogans, mounted a loud speaker on it and driven it around Rio Claro inviting people to attend Black Power marches) that his house was raided by the police when they started clamping down on opposition voices and organizations in 1970.

In 1971, in the wake of the 1970 Black Power movement, Lovelace returned to the United States, at the invitation of friends from his time at Howard University. He was invited to join in an experimental programme at Federal City College, Washington, DC (subsequently subsumed into the University of the District of Columbia), which they had designed to prepare school dropouts from underprivileged backgrounds for college. Gregory Rigsby has suggested that Lovelace's penchant for long sentences can be traced to his involvement with the use of generative grammar/rhetoric in this programme: "The long cumulative sentence, with a series of subordinating phrases and clauses, each unit taking off from a word or idea in the preceding unit, was one of the writing techniques we studied. This particular technique seems to have made a deep impression on Earl, for this style permeates *The Dragon* and *Salt*. One can open *Salt* at random and find, at least, one paragraph-long, or, at times, a page-long, sentence."[22]

But generative grammar could not have been the sole source of that style in Lovelace. His move away from the formalistic sentence structure in *The Schoolmaster* to the free-wheeling, almost unruly, style in his subsequent novels owes much to his refinement of the free-wheeling styles of the artistes (calypsonians, midnight robbers, pierrot grinnards, bookman kalinda chanters) of the bacchanal tradition.

From 1973 to 1974, Lovelace doubled as a visiting novelist and a master's student/tutor in the creative writing seminar at Johns Hopkins University, Baltimore, Maryland. He had applied to do the master of arts in creative writing seminar, was interviewed, and accepted into the programme, with a promise of some financial help. On the eve of the beginning of the programme, he was informed that the lecturer for the seminar was going away on a Fulbright fellowship and would not be available to teach it. Would he be interested in teaching the seminar? He was. He went on to lead the seminar and at the end of the academic year, he submitted the manuscript of *The Wine of Astonishment* to be assessed for his master's degree.

Although Lovelace developed a good rapport with the other students in the writing seminar and would go clubbing with them, he found the situation of being simultaneously the leader of the seminar and a student in the seminar so "awkward" that he did not tell them that he was one of them (personal interview, June 1995; Lovelace, AIP).

The group behind the curriculum development project that Lovelace went up to work with in Washington, DC, comprised mainly people with Caribbean roots, especially Trinidad and Tobago. Cognizant of the need to return to contribute to the development of the region, they had organized themselves into a discussion group, "The New Beginning" (a name suggested by Lovelace), as a platform for deliberating on the socio-political climate of the Caribbean and developing action plans to be executed on their return home. On the eve of his departure from the United States after his master's, Lovelace proposed to the membership of "The New Beginning" the idea that they should return to build a school in rural Trinidad that would not be dogmatically political, and at which members of the group would volunteer to teach in their areas of expertise and where a publishing house and, possibly, a newspaper would be established. Most, if not all, of the other members of the group were slated to return home to guaranteed jobs in the civil service, unlike Lovelace, who was returning to self-employment as a writer. They did not think his idea could be operationalized and they rejected it, causing Lovelace to lose enthusiasm in, and move away from, a group he had been instrumental in creating.

Jean and, by now, their two sons (Walt and Che) had returned home ahead of Lovelace. When Jean left the United States to return home, they were already estranged from each other so she returned to live with her mother in Rio Claro. On his return, with his utopian idea of the rural school still fresh in his mind, Lovelace decided that he wanted to live in the countryside to write and live off the land, determined to unite his training in agriculture and his career option as a writer. He mentioned his dream to a friend in Sangre Grande. The friend told him that he knew of a gentleman with such a place in Matura. Lovelace went to speak with the owner of the said property, Stephen Charles, and based on the description of the house located on the edge of a twenty-two-acre cocoa plantation, and without sight of the place, he decided to rent the house.

After making the place habitable, he invited Jean to come up from Rio Claro to see this place where he was creating the life of a writer-living-off-the-land for himself. She did. He invited her back into his life. She accepted. And together, they embarked on the creation of a life and a home in Matura that would become a go-to-place for writers and the literati, local and international, for the next ten-plus years.

By the time Lovelace went to live in Matura, he had already completed the early versions of the manuscripts of *The Wine of Astonishment* and *The Dragon Can't Dance*. Rigsby has provided an account of Lovelace working his way through the concepts that went into the making of *The Dragon Can't Dance* in a lecture he delivered in Washington, DC, titled "The Evolution of the Bad John in Trinidad".[23] At the prodding of Derek Walcott, Lovelace sent both manuscripts to Andre Deutsch. Both got positive readers' reports and were accepted for publication. But although he had finished *The Wine of*

Astonishment before *The Dragon Can't Dance*, Lovelace decided that he was not yet satisfied with *The Wine of Astonishment*: "I still wasn't satisfied with *Wine*. I said, No. And actually, I was so excited about *Dragon*, I wanted *Dragon* to come out first.... So, we decided on publishing *Dragon* first, at which point I re-wrote *Wine*" (personal interview, June 1995).

Lawrence Scott has provided a comprehensive account of the significance of the Matura home to writers, artists, and intellectuals in the 1970s and early 1980s. "An enduring memory of this time," he writes,

> was of the lanterns being lit and pumped by Earl on the dining table when we stayed well beyond dark, it getting more and more difficult to pull ourselves away from the talk which went on for hours....
>
> There were many memorable visits. Once, to River Mouth, I remember Funso Aiyejina clutching a folder of poems with the hope of meeting Derek Walcott who was up that weekend. It was the beginning of a long friendship with the then young student from Nigeria. Another time, Raffique Shah was on the beach giving us the history of 1970. There was a Sunday gathering for one of Earl's birthdays at which there was cricket in the yard. Photographs of that period bring back Merle Hodge, Norline Metivier, Wilbert Holder, and Raoul Pantin among many others, including Derek Walcott, Averil and Ken Ramchand, Marjorie Thorpe, Joan Goody, Pam Mordecai, and of course Mr. Charles ("Charlo"), who had invited Earl and Jean to come and live on the land at Francis Trace.
>
> Another of the special moments of the time we are calling Matura Days was when CLR James came to stay with us at Breakfast River and then we all moved down to Francis Trace

where Earl had invited a Parang band to play for CLR. The house was full, the yard was full. We pressed in through the Demerara windows and the half doors moving with the paranderos, their cuatros and the singing and the bottle and spoon. This music I would find threaded into the writing, feeding the rhythms of the writing – I was learning how sentences could be altered by these rhythms. Tone, Earl had already said, get the tone and you are almost there. . . .

There was always intense and incessant talk. It seems now that everything triggered a philosophical, political, or literary question.[24]

In that same essay, Scott quotes his wife, Jenny, quoting Lovelace's desire to reclaim the love and "heroism of my grandfather to be a man and to work, and of my grandmother to sell gingerbread and to take a number of her daughters' and sons' children and bring us up as hers".[25] The process of reclamation of the heroism of the ordinary citizen implicit in that desire to celebrate his grandparents would be given a grounded realization in the way Lovelace dealt with all the communities he has ever lived in. Not only did he give them life through his writing, he inserted himself into their lives and worked with them to realize their own potential. He welcomed them into his life to nurture him to live their understanding of humanity. Nowhere was this impetus better realized than in Matura.

Although Lovelace had signalled his talent for playwriting with *The New Boss* in Rio Claro in 1962, it would be his involvement with the Matura Village Council and the Matura

Folk Theatre that would provide him with the opportunity to establish himself as a serious playwright, one who was willing and able to refine aspects of the culture of the ordinary people and deploy them as bearers of themes and styles in a manner that ensures a balance between the demands of popular and literary art. *My Name Is Village*, which was written as Matura's entry for the Prime Minister's Best Village Competition of 1976, is mindful of the grading rubric for the competition. Entries were judged on dramatic storyline as well as on the use of folk music/songs and folk dances. His *Pierrot Grinnard*, a play based on a carnival character, was also Matura's entry for the competition in 1977. *My Name Is Village* won both Best Play and Best Music awards in the Prime Minister's Best Village Competition of 1976.

From the point of view of the relationship between Lovelace and his enabling community, while he is recognized as the author of the plays, the final scripts as well as their transformation into theatrical productions were collective communal undertakings. Lovelace provided the storyline and worked with the villagers to settle on the songs, dances and dialogues. The villagers also provided the bodies and the voices that activated the scripts. Many years later, Lovelace would reflect on the process for creating *My Name Is Village*: "The play came out of the village, out of Matura itself in which we began with some ideas and tried to get everybody in the play. So the play kept playing and growing and growing. . . . And it was very, very useful because it brought Matura into a feeling of itself" (personal interview, June 1995).

CHAPTER TWO

The Matura years were the "Years of Plays and Playing" for Lovelace. He wrote plays. He played football, he played cricket, he played cards, he played mas, he played himself at fetes, danced bongo at wakes and drank with the folks. Remaining true to the pattern he had established for himself in Valencia and Rio Claro (he was a member of the Valencia Village Council, 1955; member of the Rio Claro Village Council and Youth Group, 1962; and director of the Drama Group, Rio Claro, 1962), he took on several leadership roles in Matura. He was president of the village council, 1976 to 1980; president, vice-president, and public relations officer at various times in 1984; and director of the Matura Folk Theatre from 1976 to 1978. The performance of these roles allowed him to know the community and for the community to know him. During this period, he also functioned as a foundation member and president of the Trinidad and Tobago Writers Union (1976 to 1981).

In addition to the Best Village plays he wrote for the Matura Folk Theatre, Lovelace wrote two literary plays during his Matura years – *Jestina's Calypso* (based on the story of a Rio Claro neighbour and her pen pal) and *The New Hardware Store*, which picks up on the idea of identity and self-governance that he had floated in *The New Boss* but, this time, against the background of the 1970 Black Power revolution. These plays were premiered by the University of the West Indies Players in March 1978 and March 1980 respectively before subsequent international staging in several countries, including Jamaica, Guyana, the United Kingdom and Canada. Although more literary than *My Name Is Village* and *Pierrot*

Grinnard, the influence of the Best Village tradition is evident in both plays and in his stage adaptation of *The Dragon Can't Dance* and *The Wine of Astonishment*. In all of these plays, songs, especially calypsoes and/or folk songs, function as metanarratives/-narrators, echoing a similar practice in Best Village productions.

Such was Lovelace's belief in the Best Village experiment that in the early 1980s, during his attachment to the Department of English at the University of the West Indies' St Augustine campus, as a lecturer, he spearheaded the development of a creative writing course and an arts and indigenous traditions project (in collaboration with Dr Marjorie Thorpe) as academic offerings available to both undergraduates at the University of the West Indies and Best Village officers from the Culture Division of the Ministry of Community Development. He worked closely with Robyn Cross in organizing the workshops for the participants in the Arts and Indigenous Tradition project from the ministry.

The direct involvement of Lovelace in the Best Village programme at the village and national level is one example of his approach to social responsibility and mentorship. Nowhere is his mentoring spirit more evident than in his many teaching assignments over the years. Little wonder then that he has created many teacher figures in his fiction, with Alford George in *Salt* being perhaps an echo of the type of teacher/mentor that Lovelace has been.

He was the director of the fiction workshop at the Caribbean Writers' Summer Institute, University of Miami, in 1995; visiting professor in the Department of Africana

Studies, Wellesley College, Massachusetts, from 1996 to 1997; and the distinguished novelist, Department of English, Pacific Lutheran University, Tacoma, Washington. He has taught at Hartwick College, Oneonta, New York, and at Trinity College, Hartford, Connecticut. In his assessment of Lovelace's contribution to the curriculum development project in Washington, DC, Rigsby is generous in his praise of Lovelace's teaching style and pedagogy:

> His comments on students' essays were especially instructive. We shared our comments among the group. The set theory invited emphasis on structure – the essay as a set made up of subsets (interrelated paragraphs) – but Earl would not allow his students to be hemmed in. He pointed them invariably to style – word choice, sentence arrangement, and imaginative details. His students' essays, as a result, were always more lively and interesting than others that tended to be mechanically ordered and correct. In the final evaluation of our experimental curriculum, I remember the point was made that the mathematical approach to writing often stifled the students' imagination, a flaw that Earl had instinctively avoided.[26]

And Barbara Temple-Thurston, reflecting on Lovelace's impact on students at the Pacific Lutheran University, Tacoma, writes:

> Earl's service to the students he taught was the cornerstone of his presence on our campus. His gentle, laidback classroom style puzzled some students at first, but they soon realised they were in the presence of a very special person. He didn't use voicemail, didn't always check his e-mail, and wasn't always absolutely on time. But they sensed his affection for the human creature, warmed to his generous spirit, and were moved by

his insights and wisdom. His willingness to work carefully with students to find their own voice and write out of their own experience helped them all improve their writing skills, as well as grow in understanding and expression of themselves and the complex world they inhabit. His ability to bring to life the vibrant diversity of Trinidad culture opened new vistas for students, and provided bridges and opportunities never before possible. He broadened their vision with topics like cricket, Orisha, and Carnival – often supported by colourful video presentations, and with readings by Caribbean writers and thinkers. Students soon understood that they were very privileged to be taught by so renowned a writer, a view often reflected on students' evaluations of Earl's classes. . . .

Each student felt Earl's genuine interest in his or her humanity, and understood Earl's commitment to his or her progress. . . .

His affiliation with PLU has brought distinction to the university. The university's most recent alumni magazine, *Scene*, pays tribute to Earl's time at PLU, quoting the University President, Loren Anderson. Anderson recalls meeting with an educator who, upon hearing that Anderson was from "the place where Earl Lovelace teaches", immediately gave him complete attention.[27]

Lovelace is legendary for his laid-back approach to life and time referenced in the extract above. Some find this quality exasperating while others treat it as a rhythm that he would have imbibed from living and working in rural communities where it is not unusual to hear a "what's-your-rush" hurled at anyone who is in too much of a hurry. There is a 1989 story of him arriving late, very late, for the launch of his own book at the Cosmic Bookshop, West Mall, Port of Spain. Three books were being launched on that occasion, one of which was his *A Brief Conversion and Other Stories*. The other two authors were Valerie Belgrave and Marlene Philip. Only Belgrave was there for the start of the event. After an embarrassing delay, the minister of culture, Jennifer Johnson, went ahead and launched the books. Long after the ceremony, Lovelace strolled into the venue, unruffled. When the *Sunday Punch* reporter asked him why he was late, he responded: "I did not come late, the Minister left early" (*Sunday Punch*, 5 March 1989, 8).

It is instructive to note that Lovelace's lecturing forays into US universities began after his rather ambiguous relationship with the University of the West Indies, St Augustine. In addition to a number of guest appearances on the St Augustine campus in the 1970s (often through the instrumentality of Kenneth Ramchand), Lovelace functioned as a part-time lecturer in the Department of English at various points between 1979 and 1985 and, with the inception of the Campus Literature Week (1999) and the master of fine arts in creative writing – fiction (2002), he has served as writer-in-residence on three occasions. He was awarded an honorary doctor of letters by the University of the West Indies in 2002, and some of his manuscripts have been acquired by the university. But, like his relationship with Trinidad and Tobago, a country he consistently castigates for not doing enough for the welfare of its writers, his relationship with the University of the West Indies has been fraught with tension. He is critical of the university for not creating appropriate platforms for the material well-being and intellectual contribution of writers. At a personal level, he is critical of his treatment when, as a part-time lecturer, he was tardily treated: "Every June or July was a period of nervousness. . . . It was never a certainty. They didn't pay you sometimes or paid you whenever. . . . It was a very undignified thing. . . . What vexes me most about it was the contribution that I might have been able to make to the University and to the place from that location . . . couldn't be done because I couldn't accept that kind of treatment and function in that way" (personal interview, June 1995).

By the mid-1980s when Lovelace ended his sojourn in Matura and returned to Port of Spain, he had matured his world view into one that understood the complexity of the relationship between rural communities that functioned with little input from central or local government, and towns and cities with visible presence of government. He had moved from the betrayal of villagers by the schoolteacher through the betrayal of the electorate by politicians, and the failures of the Black Power revolution, to an interrogation of the dynamics of race in a multicultural society with contending racial agendas. He had arrived at his big theme and his unique narrative style: reparatory justice and narrative possession.

The economic argument for reparation, in the instance of the West Indies, has been convincingly made by Hilary McD. Beckles in *Britain's Black Debt*. But while recognizing the socio-economic rationale for reparation and the need to acknowledge the fact that New World Africans are justified in demanding reparation, Lovelace's goal in *Salt* is to drill down to the philosophical and moral implications of reparation and the centrality of reparation to all of humanity. He suggests that what makes reparation even more urgent in the case of New World Africans is the fact of the deliberate botching of emancipation, self-government and independence that were supposed to have aided their attainment of freedom but never did:

> Emancipation, self-government, and Independence never delivered their liberation to them. And while these have been important landmarks in our struggle for personhood, they never produced what the propaganda surrounding them seemed to promise. Indeed, to begin with, our acceptance of *Emancipation* as an event that fully emancipated Africans is the foundation stone of the betrayal of Africans and their hopes for the society after enslavement. It was the event that demonstrated the hesitations, and the fears the colonisers had about truly making African liberation possible, and encouraging a New World. . . .
>
> It took from 1834 to 1956 for Africans, liberated from *enslavement*, to arrive at political representation. By the time independence came in 1962, the Black leadership, that had by then come to power, did not see fit to address the omissions of the 120-odd years that had passed. . . .
>
> It took the Black Power revolt in Trinidad in 1970 to make demands for African dignity in a society over which a Black government presided. As a result of our failure to properly close accounts with that portion of our past, the resentments, the guilt, the shame, the sense of victimhood have all remained, fanned by the flames of a propaganda (coming to us from all sections of the media) that has sought to assuage the conscience

of European guilt by presenting Africans as degraded people unworthy of being accepted as fully human.[28]

Lovelace justifies his focus on the plight of New World Africans on the basis that their liberation is a base requirement in the process of the positive cultural transformation of the Caribbean:

> I believe their liberation is the key to the positive cultural transformation of the region. This should not surprise anybody since African enslavement was at the centre of the creation of the Caribbean that we know today. What I hope I have shown is that neither enslavement of Africans nor their liberation have been properly addressed, and this has prevented the various groups from evolving too far beyond the themes that preoccupied them when they first arrived in the New World. The African's central concern is still the fight against enslavement; the Indian is still obsessed with overcoming the poverty he arrived in; and the European is still embattled, building fortresses for his protection, still preoccupied with his vulnerability. I am convinced that none of these groups wants to remain in these positions. Each group wants to liberate its own creative energies and address the new concerns of the 21st century. That is why, it seems to me, we must all come together on the question of *reparation*, as the means by which we can clean the slates, and approach a new beginning.[29]

The process of reparation as articulated by Lovelace involves the coming together of victim and victimizer to repair the breaches of trust in each other in order to facilitate the liberation of each other into a new beginning. The global movement for reparation has put a dollar-and-cents price tag on it, but Lovelace's focus is on the emotional and psychological commitments that will make it possible to settle accounts, to release each group from guilt, and to create "something more affirmative to overcome the ideas of slave and slave master and nigger and coolie".[30] The one thing that Lovelace sees as engendering the affirmative spirit that will enable us to welcome each other as human beings into the New World is reparation, which he postulates as an important gesture in the process of self-humanization and the humanization of others:

> I think that when we violate another, not only do we cause them to lose something . . . we have lost something, or maybe we never had the something. When we violate someone, we have lost our respect and our love, or never knew we had them, we are lost and that is the tragedy of our arts these days, they have not been willing to talk about our profound loss, our best art has always talked about this loss, this loss that we suffer when we violate others; and I want to suggest that the act of reparation is the gesture we make to restore our loss, to declare that we have restored those lost qualities in ourselves, to steady the madness that had consumed us; the gestures that will return us to sanity, a moral sanity. It seems to me that the victim is also a participant who has come by his anger and his shame and his need for vengeance; the violated has to surrender his mistrust.[31]

Lovelace understands that what he proposes requires the re-education of both victims and victimizers. In essence, Africans should not expect reparation if they are unwilling to accept the humanity of all the other ethnic groups who share the Caribbean space with them. Similarly, no people should expect forgiveness or belonging if they refuse to take responsibility for their actions that would have caused harm to others. Through the inclusivity of his proposed reparation, Lovelace is affirming his own New World-ness, a vision that allows him to create complex characters who are at once confident and uncertain of the rightness or otherwise of their vision; characters who are constantly examining and re-examining their pasts and their options for the future; men and women who are at once very Caribbean and very universal, full of foibles and ennobling traits and, though constrained by the contradictions in their histories and contemporary life, passionately desirous of redemption: "Indeed, this is one of the main themes of *Salt*. So we have here three characters who stand for the African, European and Indian, the best of them, the most hopeful and each on behalf of their group seeks to engage the promise of the New World space, against the background of guilt and shame and opportunism and a real or imagined sense of victimhood."[32] In the specific case of Africans, he makes four concrete suggestions that could facilitate the process of their reparation: "(1) that discussions on reparation begin in society, (2) that monuments be erected to those who have struggled, (3) that the power of the state be responsible for setting the highest standards for humanity, and (4) that Black people both take back and be given back the task of constructing our own self-image."[33]

From his vantage point as a writer, Lovelace advocates the deployment of literature as a tool in the process of re-education on the need for reparation. Literature, he argues, can be used to call us to account as humans, by placing before us what we say we value and believe and by showing us how we act in regard to these beliefs and values. It demonstrates our heroism, our courage and all our virtues, but it also displays our hypocrisy, our arrogance, our injustice, our errors, and our stupidity. . . . And what literature does is to show us ourselves and help us to understand our situation, acknowledge our flaws and redeem ourselves.[34]

Lovelace reaffirms that the "failure to accord Africans any compensation for the violations they had suffered was bad enough" but that what "was worse was that they were set at liberty into a society where they were to be treated with gross inequality".[35] And it is for that reason that he is demanding reparation. The African case is a test case, not the only case. Nowhere in his argument does he suggest that reparation is due only to Africans. In essence, to affirm that black lives matter does not negate the fact that other lives matter.

THREE

Content is important but so too is style. Not style as adornment but style as substance. Most of Lovelace's writerly struggles over the years have been framed by his desire to find the best style for telling the stories he has committed to tell. For this enterprise, he has chosen to mine the submerged cultures of the New World African for pointers and templates for his own aesthetics. His choice is set against the background of his analysis of the African cultural terrain as the foundational/base culture of the New World of the Caribbean. He argues that, as a result of the almost total annihilation of Amerindians and their culture, the spiritual and psychological detachment of European colonizers from the Caribbean landscape, and the significant cultural concessions grudgingly granted to indentured Indians that enabled them to engage with their new landscape with significant components of the ethos of their religious rituals, African culture, which was forced to reinvent itself because of its forced separation from its roots, has inevitably emerged as the foundational impulse of what would eventually constitute Caribbean folk culture and consciousness:

CHAPTER THREE

> It would be these Africans who would constitute the Caribbean folk, because, more than the Europeans then, or any of the indentured servants that were to follow, their condition of enslavement and their reality of being cut off from their homeland gave them no alternative but to make the Caribbean their home. And while the Europeans also lived in the Caribbean, they lived in constant reference to Europe, drawing from it physical and psychological support. There was no reason for them to become Caribbean in anything but residence. Their European-ness was their authorisation. They had no need to create. They would extend Europe; they would not create a Caribbean for itself. What folk culture we have was created by those enslaved Africans.[36]

In the cultural essays in *Growing in the Dark*, Lovelace identifies and exalts various aspects of New World African culture. He celebrates dance as one of the artistic ways in which enslaved New World Africans affirmed and celebrated their power and control over their bodies; he draws attention to the instruments used for making the music to which the enslaved Africans danced (drums; tambour bamboo, which replaced the banned drum; steelpan, which evolved from the tambour bamboo as evidence of the ingenuity of the New World African); he reclaims and centre-stages folk religion, especially Orisa and Spiritual Baptist; and he analyses carnival as a festival that began as a French Creole celebration but which had been appropriated and transformed by Africans into a vessel for the manifestation and interrogation of all elements of their New World existence. He reconceptualizes and narrates carnival as a festival that contains examples of the influence of various African dance traditions (limbo, stickfight, bongo dance steps and the dances of possession). He identifies the influence of African singing traditions in carnival, from the satirical and secular style of protest calypsoes through the semi-religious style of a David Rudder to the fully religious style of an Ella Andall. He draws attention to the centrality of the drum language of pan, whose defining spirit derives from the rhythms of the Orisa tradition. He envisions the indigenous traditions of Trinidad and Tobago as alternative inscriptions of history, which would form valuable sources of, and resources for, his aesthetics. He embraces carnival as the one ritual in which all the cultural dynamics that make up the New World African experience have congregated to interact. The question for Lovelace is, if the ordinary people have succeeded in reinterpreting themselves into their New World realities, how does the writer tap into their ingenuity? His answer is to deploy the recreated New World cultures into metanarrative language/signifiers with which to reinterpret the people back to themselves. His resolve has led him to create novels that are so suffused with the rhythm of the people that they are practically singing novels, hence the tag of novelypso attached to them. It is interesting that the child who grew up in a house in Tobago where he was forbidden to sing calypso, where nobody played mas, and where carnival was considered an activity of the devil, would not only grow up to embrace African culture, especially carnival, but to mine it for his aesthetics.

With *While Gods Are Falling* (1965), Lovelace signals an interest in carnival and its related traditions as containing aspects that could be deployed as aids to narration. He employs calypso, stick fighting and mas to create the atmosphere in this novel. Through his narration of the protagonist's carnival route through Port of Spain, Lovelace takes us on a Joycean tour of the city. By *The Wine of Astonishment* (1982), he has started the process of complicating his narrative codes. He exhibits characteristics unique to the chantwell of the calypso tradition in the person of Mother Eva, the first-person narrator of the novel, a narrative habit that will grow incrementally until we arrive at the self-declaring calypsonian/midnight robber in *Is Just a Movie* ("My name is Kangkala [aka King Kala], maker of confusion, recorder of gossip, destroyer of reputations, seeker of secrets" [5]). Also, the rebellious spirit of Bolo (the stick fighter) and the resistance ethos of the besieged African spirituality of the Spiritual Baptist faith both converge to be channelled, at the end of *The Wine of Astonishment*, through the sound of the steel band, another integral component of carnival.

The Dragon Can't Dance, with its acknowledgement of calypso, pan and mas, is the quintessential carnival novel. With this novel, Lovelace established himself as a sensitive, perceptive and rigorous interrogator and manipulator of carnival and the carnivalesque for thematic and aesthetic purposes. The overall structure of *The Dragon Can't Dance* approximates the movement from pre-carnival through carnival Monday and Tuesday to post-carnival/Ash Wednesday. The events leading up to the confrontation between the Gang of Nine and the police parallel a build-up to carnival; the actual confrontation (appropriately titled "The Dragon Dance", which presents Fisheye, Aldrick and the others "playing themselves") matches carnival proper (little wonder that Fisheye would later say in prison: "We really play a mas', eh, Aldrick? You couldn't play a better dragon"); and the prison phase signifies post-carnival/Ash Wednesday, the traditional state of hangover and reflection (*Dragon*, 186).

In his use of the dragon mas as a central motif, Lovelace not only echoes the sacred snake among many West African peoples, but also acknowledges the long and complex struggles of Calvary Hill/New World Africans against oppression, and stimulates a visual image of carnival revellers winding their way through the streets of Port of Spain. But more importantly, both from the point of view of ideology and style, when Aldrick inhabits the dragon and the dragon inhabits Aldrick, Lovelace is invoking the masking traditions of Africa where masking is a death-defying, death-defeating ritual, a metaphor for the conquest of death and the past, a renewable memory charm/chip for warding off amnesia. In Africa, through masking, ancestors visit to re/establish and re/validate connections; the carnival that accompanies their re/emergence functions as the occasion for the in/gathering of the tribe (exiles return to re/validate their psychic links with both community and ancestors; and important clan meetings are scheduled for this season to facilitate inter/action between re/activated ancestors, returning exiles and the stay-at-home). This dimension of African masking tradition is also evident in New World carnivals, which witness the homecoming of many and the re/activation and/or re/validation of relationships. This socio-psychic possibility in carnival coincides with Lovelace's assertion that "carnival is like a community embracing itself. Embracing each other in order to ward off the fears of tomorrow. Or the fear of death. It is a kind of catharsis through which we all gain strength from each other because everybody is immortal. Everybody is beautiful. And one joins in to become immortal and beautiful as well."[37] In essence, carnival creates the same kind of immortality that literature engenders.

By the time we get to *Salt*, Lovelace is in full aesthetic flight. The overall phrasing of *Salt*, like that of carnival, is informed by the need to acknowledge ancestral energies as central tropes in the historical, contemporary and future realities of the Caribbean. Bango tells stories of past struggles to Travey, his nephew, who, in turn, tells them to the reader, thus validating the historical legacies of Bango's ancestors, of Bango himself, of the narrator and his family, of Alford, his teacher, and of the community as a whole. In essence, the historical imagination at work here is one that acknowledges the power of mask/literature over death, history and amnesia; it is an imagination that recognizes the iconic implications of ancestor veneration, a notion underscored in *The Dragon Can't Dance* through Aldrick's perception of his dragon-making/-carrying/-dancing role as that of the activator of the past and the recorder of the material and spiritual history and the contemporary realities of his people. Every year, when he engages in the construction of his dragon costume, Aldrick becomes the priest and enters into a ritualistic narration of *his* history and *his* people:

> In truth, it was in a spirit of priesthood that Aldrick addressed his work; for, the making of his dragon costume was to him always a new miracle, a new test not only of his skill but of his faith. . . .
>
> Aldrick worked slowly, deliberately; and every thread he sewed, every scale he put on the body of the dragon, was a thought, a gesture, an adventure, a name that celebrated some part of his journey to and his surviving upon this hill. . . . [H]e sewed scales for his grandfather, who he remembered from the far distance of his boyhood on that browning green hill between the giant immortelle trees above the cocoa and dying bananas. (*Dragon*, 36–37)

The personal history in the above anticipates and complements the collective history that the ritual of jouvay awakens in Calvary Hill:

> Up on the Hill Carnival Monday morning breaks on the backs of these thin shacks with no cock's crow, and before the mist clears, little boys, costumed in old dresses, their heads tied, holding brooms made from the ribs of coconut palm leaves, blowing whistles and beating kerosene tins for drums, move across the face of the awakening Hill, sweeping yards in a ritual, heralding the masqueraders' coming, that goes back centuries for its beginnings, back across the Middle Passage, back to Mali and to Guinea and Dahomey and Congo, back to Africa. (*Dragon*, 120)

The function of Aldrick, the mas maker, as a re-memberer of personal and collective histories, coincides with that of the writer as an autobiographer and a biographer. Like Aldrick, Lovelace is constantly secreting autobiographical and biographical materials (about people and the nation) in his work. In *The Dragon Can't Dance*, the grandfather figure in Aldrick's re-creation is Lovelace's fictional activation of his maternal grandfather who "was stern, stiff and very proud" (36). This process of recall is the writerly equivalent of the ritual recall of ancestors into our lives and, ironically, also an echo of the ritual invocation of the living into our prayers and hopes to wish them well, like Lovelace the child on the Scarborough hospital bed, who was certain he was going to die, a victim of typhoid, but alert and perceptive enough to recite the names of his relatives, to remember and wish them well.

In addition to writers' deployment of autobiographical details in creating fictions, they can also deploy front matters as narrative tools. Of the two major front matters, acknowledgements are usually self-explanatory but not so dedications. In the particular instance of Lovelace, unless you know who Aunt Lorna was in his life, the part dedication of *While Gods Are Falling* to her will not yield its total meaning. But once the reader becomes privy to her story, it becomes clear that the dedication was Lovelace's way of offering a mea culpa for his betrayal of her in 1948 when he chose his mother over her. The remorse becomes even more profound against the background of this being his first published book. Jean and his children are "repeat offenders" on his dedication pages. No surprise there. You can track the size of his family at the time of publication of each book by the number of his children listed on the dedication pages. Apart from Aunt Lorna, the other family members who earned dedications are his sisters,

Lillian and Lyris, both of whom played critical roles in his upbringing, before and after the death of their mother. Then there are the benefactors, especially Stephen Charles of Matura, from whom he rented the now-famous Francis Trace house and land, and Bob Benson, who invited him to teach at Hartwick College at a financially challenging time in his life. And there are the lovers. And his many friends, some of whom, like Lawrence and Jenny Scott, are also "repeat offenders". *The Schoolmaster* is partly dedicated to "my friends at the 'college' at Valencia". That dedication reminds me of a road trip I took with him in 2004, a dry run of the journey through his literary landscape that was a major part of his seventieth birthday celebrations in 2005. When we got to Valencia, he pointed to a rum shop and said, with his characteristic laughter in his throat, "That is the university I went to." Alas, the rum shop has since been converted into an American fast-food place.

The danger with dedications is that a writer hardly writes enough books in his or her lifetime to have enough dedication pages for all who may be important and deserving in his or her life. Especially, if like Lovelace, you have been blessed with many friends and family members. Anyway, not to worry, Lovelace has a unique solution to that problem. At the climax of *Salt*, he populates the independence march led by Bango with Bango's fellow fictional characters as well as with his own real-life friends and collaborators in a grand acknowledgement of their friendship and their contribution to the struggle for the creation of a new Caribbean society. It is very easy to see this as gimmickry, as a cute way to provide a conversation piece – an "Eh, boy, I see you is in the Lovelace book. You reach, boy!" But such an interpretation will be ignoring the dynamics of the bacchanal tradition that Lovelace has mined for style. The bacchanal tradition is one in which the boundaries between fiction/religion/the imaginary and reality, between life and death, between the past and the present, and between the visible and the invisible can be unstable. Such boundaries are candidates for dissolution, once the ritual conditions are right. A recognition of the instability and dissolubility of intermediate realms emboldens Lovelace to insert us into our fiction and our fiction into our life in what is essentially a fictive visualization of the "las' lap", that liberal and unregimented twilight hour and space on carnival Tuesday night when masqueraders (fictional characters) and spectators (friends, family and collaborators) merge into one charged body of humanity to celebrate life in anticipation of the sober realities of Ash Wednesday. In the deftness of Lovelace's bacchanal imagination, the message has become the style and the style has become the message.

In *Salt*, Lovelace refines the obliteration of the chasm between the language of narration and the language of interaction, between the language of oppression and the language of liberation, and between the language of pain and the language of relief. He evolves an inclusive philosophy of welcoming each other into the physical and psychic spaces of the New World, guided by an aesthetic that is grounded in, and directed by, the complexity of the submerged histories of the land. He takes the notion of narrative alchemy to a new level as he searches for a way to "deal with the number of voices wanting to speak" by developing a democratic narrative style capable of evoking "voices from the past to tell their story, as well as have the people of all ethnic groups who were involved in the dramas tell theirs".[38] Faced with a carnival of contending races, histories, sensibilities and agendas, Lovelace finally arrives at a convincing multi-vocal and multi-perspective narrator/narrative. For this feat, he has borrowed his template (narrative possession) from African traditions, especially the rituals of the Orisa and Spiritual Baptist faiths.

As a novel about the many stories of the New World, *Salt* raises questions about how much of the content of a story originates solely in the consciousness of the storyteller and/or the community, and how much of the consciousness of a story or the power of the events in the story invades the consciousness of the storyteller and, by extension, forces him or her to tell a particular story in a particular way at a particular moment in time. As a means of suggesting the complex relationship among the story, the storyteller and the contending perceptions of history, reality and orality inherent in the story, Lovelace adopts the use of multiple narrative voices and mixed narrative patterns. Additionally, he employs a multi-vocal, sublimated overarching first-person narrator who is substantially stripped of his own ego, and is regularly possessed and deployed by other characters who force him to reiterate their visions and their specific versions and consciousness of the/their stories. This narrative technique approximates the behaviour of the medium in Orisa and other Africa-inspired rituals (as well as all rituals in which possession forms a part of the process) who loses his or her voice and personality and is inhabited by, and sublimated to, the voice and distinctive personality traits of the possessing/mounting deity. Hence, in spite of the desire of his mother to steer him clear of Uncle Bango and his stories, the narrator in *Salt*, like a finely primed Orisa medium under the irresistible control of the mounting deity, is constantly ridden by Uncle Bango's stories and the ancestral memories lodged in them. The narrator becomes the living voice of the future possessed and controlled by the vision of the present and the past. He is the medium possessed by, and voicing the complete continuum of, human civilization.

Lovelace's lifelong advocacy that people must not surrender control to their leaders, but rather get involved in the politics and governance, finds aesthetic expression in the way the human subjects of the various stories in *Salt* occasionally exercise their option to stroll into their stories and take over the narration from the narrator. In essence, if an advocate is underperforming, the owner of the case must exercise the option to step into the narration, take it over and demonstrate how he or she would like his or her story to be told.

In *Salt*, with his obliteration of the distinction between third-person and first-person narrations/narrators and a focus on mixed narrative patterns, as well as the possession of the narrators by both stories and the subject of the stories, Lovelace arrives at a technique that, though risky, is versatile enough to articulate the complexities of the Caribbean psyche and the multiple strands at the core of Caribbean civilization.

If Lovelace's novels often yield more meaning than their lengths tend to suggest, it is because he has found deft ways to deploy aspects of the bacchanal tradition as signifiers that can function as (1) *direct narrative threads* (Philo's calypsoes in *The Dragon Can't Dance*); (2) *explicit complementary narrative threads* (Spoiler's "Himself Tell Himself" in *While Gods Are Falling;* stickfighting in *The Wine of Astonishment* and *The Dragon Can't Dance*); (3) *implicit complementary narrative threads* (Sparrow's "Ten to One is Murder" in the Bolo/Prince confrontation); and/or (4) *implicit contrasting narrative threads* (Miss Myrtle's retort to Sparrow's "The Yankees Gone" in *Salt*). Similarly, by their very nature, his unidentified calypsonian-narrator in *The Dragon Can't Dance* (he echoes the African masked ancestral figure whose very mask is what gives him the authority and protection to speak the truth to all) and the mutative/possessed/shape-shifting narrators in *Salt* all become ideal vessels for the expression of the complementary/contradictory omens in a multicultural and multifaceted Caribbean.

Lovelace's journey to this point of aesthetic crystallization and illumination has been informed and directed by his conscious and unconscious location in some of the many liminal zones in the Caribbean, especially in Trinidad and Tobago, as a multicultural construct. George Lamming has observed that "a whole planet collapsed in this Archipelago: Europe, Africa, Asia, and the ancient ecology of diverse Amerindian ancestry".[39] Lovelace has drilled down into the crystals formed from that fusion of the many worlds in the Caribbean and has concluded:

CHAPTER THREE

> The Caribbean is the nucleus of the New World Civilisation, the view here being that the coming together in these islands by people from the old world to meet people of the New World in conditions of servitude, of rebellion, of power, was all geared to the New World challenge. Trinidad is one of the centres of this New World since it is the place where all these things have come together through songs, by migration, by settlement of people from other islands. How do you reclaim the light? . . . If Naipaul's thesis was that the British had created nothing in the West Indies, I am looking to see what we had created, as in Carnival, and how we enter the world. How do we speak to the world? Speak for the world?[40]

Lovelace occupies the liminal zone between the major races in Trinidad and Tobago. In addition to his own racial heritage that is an amalgamation of African, Amerindian and Spanish, he was married to an Indian. With a Trinidadian father and a Tobagonian mother, he identifies with the ampersand that sits, a barely-able-to-crawl-child, between Trinidad & Tobago, uncertain of its role and power in the union. At every point in his development as a person and as a writer, Lovelace has been mindful of the ambiguity and complexity inherent in the New World, even as he self-identifies with suppressed cultures and peoples. In one response to compliments often paid to him for his maroon courage in living and working out of the Caribbean, for remaining dedicated to the hope and newness of the region despite the grim realities of the place, Lovelace reflects that "it is that reality that shaped me. People act as if there is another reality."[41]

Actually, there *are* other realities. Like exile, physical or psychological. But, it just so happened that the power of events conspired to impose the embrace of home on a willing Lovelace:

> This is the reality I know, born in colonialism, shaped by reading, educated by the people of the countryside, the people at the corners, in the rum shops, by the wappie table, on the cricket and football fields. This is the reality that we have to make into a home and a place of delight and these are the people with whom we have to sup and play and love. If I am wedded to these people, if I am respectful of them and celebratory of them and defensive of them, it is because they are who I know. Indeed, they are who I am. And my task is to help make us self-confident and to help us to discover the first-class humans that, in our hearts, we are.[42]

That ideological choice (literary and thematic) is what we celebrate when we celebrate Lovelace as the committed artist. Ralph de Boissière, writing from Australia, puts it best in a letter to Lovelace dated 19 May 1984, praising him for the success of *The Dragon Can't Dance*: "What must surely impress anyone about your book is the tenderness you bear within yourself towards our people. This is rare and to be treasured at a time in history when human life has no value. . . . It is a book I will read again, and if I say so you can be sure I think highly of it."

Mr Nelson was wrong. The sadhu was right. Earl Wilbert Lovelace has been good for his world.

NOTES

1. For a detailed account of the week-long national celebrations, see Aiyejina, "Narrating the Narrator", 1–6.
2. Lovelace, "From De I-lands", in Aiyejina, *Growing*, 2.
3. Ibid., 3.
4. Ibid., 2.
5. Ibid., 3–4.
6. Lovelace, "Working Obeah", in Aiyejina, *Growing*, 222.
7. Ibid., 222–23.
8. Ibid., 223.
9. Lovelace, "A Glimpse of the Future", in Aiyejina, *Growing*, 211.
10. Aiyejina, "Novelypso", 103–19.
11. "A Manicou Hunt" (Earl Lovelace Manuscripts, Alma Jordan Library, University of the West Indies, St Augustine, Box 22, Folder 20).
12. Lovelace, "Involvement Is the People's Only Guarantee", in Aiyejina, *Growing*, 129–30.
13. See pp. 14, 16, 34, 35, 36 and 37 of the *Frog Hopper* (May 1962) for comments on Lovelace by his fellow students and a record of his athletic achievements as a student at Centeno.
14. Lovelace, "The Ongoing Value of Our Indigenous Traditions", in Aiyejina, *Growing*, 30–31.
15. Lovelace, "Caribbean Folk Culture within the Process of Modernisation", in Aiyejina, *Growing*, 27.
16. Lovelace, "The Ongoing Value of Our Indigenous Traditions", in Aiyejina, *Growing*, 30–37.

17. Ibid., 32.
18. Lovelace, "In the Dance", in Aiyejina, *Growing*, 187–88.
19. Lovelace, "Engaging the World", in Aiyejina, *Growing*, 152.
20. "Another Stranger Home"/"A Lion on the Street" and "Melville" (Earl Lovelace Manuscripts, Alma Jordan Library, University of the West Indies, St Augustine, Box 15 Folders 5 and 7).
21. Rigsby, "Earl Lovelace's Years", 149.
22. Ibid., 148.
23. Ibid., 147.
24. Scott, "Matura Days", 154–55.
25. Ibid., 156.
26. Rigsby, "Earl Lovelace's Years", 148.
27. Temple-Thurston, "Earl Lovelace at PLU", 151–52.
28. Lovelace, "Welcoming Each Other: Cultural Transformation of the Caribbean in the 21st Century", in Aiyejina, *Growing*, 167–68.
29. Ibid., 163.
30. Lovelace, "Artists as Agents of Unity", in Aiyejina, *Growing*, 100.
31. Lovelace, "Reparation: For and From Whom?", in Aiyejina, *Growing*, 181.
32. Aiyejina, "Earl Lovelace", 8.
33. Lovelace, "Welcoming Each Other", in Aiyejina, *Growing*, 173.
34. Lovelace, "Reparation: For and from Whom?", in Aiyejina, *Growing*, 182.
35. Ibid., 179.
36. Lovelace, "Caribbean Folk Culture within the Process of Modernisation", in Aiyejina, *Growing*, 26.
37. Sisto, "Edith Pérez Sisto Talks with Earl Lovelace".
38. Aiyejina, "Earl Lovelace", 2.
39. Lamming, *Enterprise of the Indies*, vi–viii.
40. Lovelace, "Working Obeah", in Aiyejina, *Growing*, 226.
41. Lovelace, "They Ask", 162.
42. Ibid.

BIBLIOGRAPHY

Aiyejina, Funso. "African Possession Rituals in the Novels of Earl Lovelace". *Journal of African Roots* 1, no. 1 (2001): 15–17.

———. "Earl Lovelace". In *Self Portraits: Interviews with Ten West Indian Writers and Two Critics*, 1–22. St Augustine, Trinidad: School of Continuing Studies, University of the West Indies, 2003.

———. "Earl Lovelace: A Chronology". *Anthurium* 4, no. 2 (Fall 2006). http://www.academia.edu/9609901/Earl_Lovelace_A_Chronology.

———, ed. *Growing in the Dark: Selected Essays*. San Juan, Trinidad: Lexicon Trinidad, 2003.

———. "Lovelace's Prospect: Masquerade or Masquerader?" *Trinidad and Tobago Review* 16, nos. 7–9 (September 1994): 7–10.

———. "Myth, Memory and Masks: Sankofa Aesthetics in Wole Soyinka, August Wilson, and Earl Lovelace". In *Gem of the Ocean: Essays on August Wilson in the Black Diaspora*, edited by Ọlásopé O. Oyèláràn and Kwame S. Dawes, 93–106. Chicago: Third World Press, 2015.

———. "Narrating the Narrator: An Occasion for Celebration". In *A Place in the World: Essays and Tributes in Honour of Earl Lovelace @ 70*, edited by Funso Aiyejina, 1–6. Caroni, Trinidad: Lexicon Trinidad, 2008.

———. "Novelypso: Earl Lovelace and the Bacchanal Tradition". In *A Place in the World: Essays and Tributes in Honour of Earl Lovelace*

@ 70, edited by Funso Aiyejina, 103–19. Caroni, Trinidad: Lexicon Trinidad, 2008.

———. "Novelypso: Indigenous Narrative Strategies in Earl Lovelace's Fiction". *Trinidad and Tobago Review* 22, nos. 7–8 (August 2000): 15–17.

———. "*Salt*: A Complex Tapestry". *Trinidad and Tobago Review* 18, nos. 10–12 (1996): 13–16.

———. "Unmasking the Chantwell Narrator in Earl Lovelace's Fiction". In *Music, Memory, Resistance: Calypso and the Caribbean Literary Imagination*, edited by Sandra Pouchet Paquet, Patricia J. Saunders, and Stephen Stuempfle, 151–62. Kingston: Ian Randle, 2007.

Beckles, Hilary McD. *Britain's Black Debt*. Kingston: University of the West Indies Press, 2013.

Brown, Wayne. "The Restlessness of Earl Lovelace: Part One". *Trinidad Guardian*, 2 July 1984, 9.

———. "Lovelace: The Social Radical: Conclusion". *Trinidad Guardian*, 3 July 1984, 7.

Cooper, Carolyn. "Critical Introduction". In *The Dragon Can't Dance*, by Earl Lovelace, 9–21. London: Longman, 1988.

Dance, Daryl Cumber. "Earl Lovelace". In *Fifty Caribbean Writers: A Bio-Bibliographical Critical Sourcebook*, edited by Daryl Cumber Dance, 276–83. New York: Greenwood, 1986.

"Earl Lovelace". In *Major 20th-Century Writers: A Selection of Sketches from Contemporary Authors*, edited by Bryan Ryan, 1823. Detroit: Gale Research, 1991.

"Earl Lovelace". In *New World Adams: Conversations with Contemporary West Indian Writers*, edited by Daryl Cumber Dance, 145–57. Leeds: Peepal Tree.

"Earl Lovelace". In *World Authors, 1985–1990*, edited by Vineta Colby, 509–11. New York: Wilson, 1995.

Earl Lovelace: A Writer in His Place. Directed by Funso Aiyejina, 2014. Arouca, Trinidad: Alfaa Projects, 2014. DVD.

Harney, Stefano. "Beyond Nationalism: Literary Nation-Building in the Work of Earl Lovelace and Michael Anthony". In *Nationalism and Identity: Culture and the Imagination in a Caribbean Diaspora*, edited by Stefano Harney, 31–51. Kingston: University of the West Indies Press, 2006.

Harris, Jennifer. "Earl Lovelace Biography". In *Brief Biographies: Contemporary Novelists*, vol. 11. http://biography.jrank.org/pages/4539/Lovelace-Earl.html.

Hewson, Kelly. "An Interview with Earl Lovelace, June 2003". *Postcolonial Text* 1, no. 1 (2004). http://postcolonial.org/index.php/pct/article/view/344/802.

Hodge, Merle. "Earl Lovelace and the Evolution of Voice in the History of the Novel in Trinidad and Tobago". PhD dissertation, University of the West Indies, St Augustine, 2005.

Joebell and America. Directed by Asha Lovelace and Earl Lovelace. 2004. Port of Spain, Trinidad: Caribbean Communications Network Six Point Production, 2004. DVD.

Juneja, Renu. "Spirited Bodies in Earl Lovelace's *The Wine of Astonishment*". In *Reading the Social Body*, edited by Catherine B. Burroughs and Jeffrey David Ehrenreich, 202–17. Iowa City: University of Iowa Press, 1993.

———. "Culture and Identity in Lovelace's *The Wine of Astonishment*". In *Imagination, Emblems and Expressions: Essays on Latin American, Caribbean, and Continental Culture and Identity*, edited by Helen Ryan-Ransom, 193–212. Bowling Green, OH: Popular Press, 1993.

Lamming, George, ed. *Enterprise of the Indies*. Tunapuna, Trinidad: Trinidad and Tobago Institute of the West Indies, 1999.

Lichenstein, David P. "A Brief Biography of Earl Lovelace". Postcolonial Web: Earl Lovelace. 1999. http://www.postcolonialweb.org/caribbean/lovelace/bio.html.

Lovelace, Earl. *A Brief Conversion and Other Stories*. Caribbean Writers Series. London: Heinemann, 1988.

———. "Calypso and the Bacchanal Connection". In *Music, Memory, Resistance: Calypso and the Caribbean Literary Imagination*, edited by Sandra Pouchet Paquet, Patricia J. Saunders and Stephen Stuempfle, 139–50. Kingston: Ian Randle, 2007.

———. *Crawfie the Crapaud*. Harlow, UK: Longman, 1997.

———. *The Dragon Can't Dance*. London: Andre Deutsch, 1979.

———. "Fools". *Frog Hopper* (May 1962): 20–23.

———. *Is Just a Movie*. London: Faber and Faber, 2011.

———. *Jestina's Calypso and Other Plays*. London: Heinemann, 1984.

———. *Salt*. London: Faber and Faber, 1996.

———. *The Schoolmaster*. London: Collins, 1968.

———. "They Ask: Why Did I Remain? Not for the Applauding Rain . . .". In *A Place in the World: Essays and Tributes in Honour of Earl Lovelace @ 70*, edited by Funso Aiyejina, 161–62. Caroni, Trinidad: Lexicon Trinidad, 2008.

———. *While Gods Are Falling*. London: Collins, 1965.

———. *The Wine of Astonishment*. London: Andre Deutsch, 1982.

"Lovelace, Earl". In *Cambridge Guide to Literature in English*, 3rd ed., edited by Dominic Head. Cambridge: Cambridge University Press, 2006.

Mahabir, Kumar. *The Indian in a Black World: The Indian Presence in Earl Lovelace's "The Dragon Can't Dance."* Carapichaima, Trinidad: Indian Review Committee, Caribbean Institute of Indian Studies and Research, [198?].

———. "The Indian Presence in Lovelace's *Dragon*". *Daily Express* (section 3), 1 November 2005: 2–3, 5, 6, 9, 11, 13, 15, 17–19, 21, 23.

Quamina-Aiyejina, Lynda. "Earl Lovelace: Bibliography of Primary and Secondary Works". In *A Place in the World: Essays and Tributes in Honour of Earl Lovelace @ 70*, edited by Funso Aiyejina, 165–95. Caroni, Trinidad: Lexicon Trinidad, 2008.

Ramchand, Kenneth. "Calling All Dragons: The Crumbling of Caribbean Masculinity". In *Interrogating Caribbean Masculinities: Theoretical and Empirical Analyses*, edited by Rhoda Reddock, 309–25. Kingston: University of the West Indies Press, 2004.

———. Introduction to *The Schoolmaster*, by Earl Lovelace, v–xvii. London: Heinemann, 1979.

Reyes, Angelita. " 'All o' We Is One': Or, Carnival as Ritual of Resistance: *The Dragon Can't Dance*". In *African Literature in Its Social and Political Dimensions*, edited by Eileen Julien, Mildred Mortimer and Curtis Schade, 59–68. Annual Selected Papers of the African Literature Association, no. 9. Washington, DC: Three Continents, 1986.

Rigsby, Gregory. "Earl Lovelace's Years in Washington, DC: A Personal Memoir". In *A Place in the World: Essays and Tributes in Honour of Earl Lovelace @ 70*, edited by Funso Aiyejina, 147–50. Caroni, Trinidad: Lexicon Trinidad, 2008.

Rohlehr, Gordon. "Earl Lovelace's New World of the Caribbean". In *A Place in the World: Essays and Tributes in Honour of Earl Lovelace @ 70*, edited by Funso Aiyejina, 9–35. Caroni, Trinidad: Lexicon Trinidad, 2008.

Schwarz, Bill, ed. *Caribbean Literature after Independence: The Case of Earl Lovelace*. London: Institute for the Study of the Americas, University of London, 2008.

Scott, Lawrence. "Matura Days: A Memoir (for Earl)". In *A Place in the World: Essays and Tributes in Honour of Earl Lovelace @ 70*, edited by Funso Aiyejina, 153–58. Caroni, Trinidad: Lexicon Trinidad, 2008.

Sisto, Edith Pérez. "Edith Pérez Sisto Talks with Earl Lovelace". *Trinidadian Letters*, http://www.geocities.com. Accessed March 2007.

Stone, Judy S. "The Mass Appeal of the Musical: Roderick Walcott, Earl Lovelace". In *Theatre: Studies in West Indian Literature*, by Judy S. Stone, 71–90. London: Macmillan, 1994.

Temple-Thurston, Barbara. "Earl Lovelace at PLU". In *A Place in the World: Essays and Tributes in Honour of Earl Lovelace @ 70*, edited by Funso Aiyejina, 151–52. Caroni, Trinidad: Lexicon Trinidad, 2008.

Thompson-Cager, Chezia. "Earl Lovelace". In *Concise Dictionary of World Literary Biography*. Vol. 3: *African, Caribbean, and Latin American Writers*, 360–68. Detroit, MI: Gale Research, 2000.

———. "Earl Lovelace". In *Twentieth-Century Caribbean and Black African Writers*, edited by Bernth Lindfors and Reinhard Sander, 70–77. Dictionary of Literary Biography, vol. 125. Detroit, MI: Gale Research, 1993.

———. "Earl Lovelace's Bad Johns, Street Princes, and the Masters of Schools". In *Imagination, Emblems and Expressions: Essays on Latin American, Caribbean, and Continental Culture and Identity*, edited by Helen Ryan-Ransom, 213–29. Bowling Green, OH: Popular Press, 1993.

Thorpe, Marjorie. "In Search of the West Indian Hero: A Study of Earl Lovelace's Fiction". *Trinidad and Tobago Review* 6, no. 3 (Back to School 1982): 12–13, 18, 21.

———. Introduction to *The Wine of Astonishment*, by Earl Lovelace, vii–xiv. London: Heinemann, 1982.

ACKNOWLEDGEMENTS

I would like to start by thanking Earl Lovelace for giving me access to his papers, especially his autobiography-in-progress, and for granting me many hours of formal and informal interview sessions. I wish, too, to thank his children Walt, Che, Lulu, Maya, Tiy and Chiedu for their support, and to single out Lulu for helping to source some crucial materials for this project and Walt for permission to use his picture of their dad.

This book would not have been possible without the many conversations with friends and colleagues over the years. My thanks go out to Carolyn Allen, Jim Armstrong, Margaret Busby, Carolyn Cooper, Eddie Hernandez, John Wayne Fortune, Merle Hodge, Barbara Jenkins, Jean Lovelace, Lyris Lovelace, Jennifer Rahim, Kenneth Ramchand, Louis Regis, Gordon Rohlehr, Jenny and Lawrence Scott, Eintou Springer, Barbara Temple-Thurston, Marjorie Thorpe, and Rose-Ann Walker. Most of the ideas in this book were first floated in the Advanced Seminar on West Indian Literature (Earl Lovelace) course at the St Augustine campus of the University

ACKNOWLEDGEMENTS

of the West Indies, which I taught for many years. I would like to thank the generations of students in that course for their engaging spirit. Special thanks to Vernette Woods, Rhoda Bharath and Lovell Francis, who, in addition to being my students, subsequently worked with me as research assistants at different stages in my career at the University of the West Indies, St Augustine, Trinidad and Tobago.

I also thank the staff of the West Indiana and Special Collections Division at the Alma Jordan Library, the University of the West Indies, St Augustine, especially Keeno Gonzales, Jonathan Hazard, Lorraine Nero and Maud Marie Sisnette for facilitating my access to the Earl Lovelace Manuscripts.

I wish also to thank Linda Speth (former director of the University of the West Indies Press) and Professor Sir Hilary Beckles (former chair of the Board of Directors of the University of the West Indies Press) for their passionate dedication to the idea of the Caribbean Biography Series, and for including Earl Lovelace on the list of the first group in the series. I would also like to thank Shivaun Hearne for making the editorial process a pleasant experience.

Thanks to my "How-the-book-going?" friends: Gene Francis, Mother Vera Francois, Nailah Folami Imoja, Adedoja Labinjo, Marina Salandy-Brown and Vera Washington.

I remain most grateful for the constant support from Ararimeh, Abuenameh and Lynda. Lynda, I could not have wished for a better mother for our children and a more perceptive intellectual companion for myself. I thank you, as always.

CPSIA information can be obtained
at www.ICGtesting.com
Printed in the USA
LVHW091715190119
604530LV00001B/6/P